MOVING WITH THE BROKEN CIRCLE OF TIME

Too often I am tempted to believe that my life is an orderly process that means something and is headed somewhere. I pace myself against some ideal of how far I should have come by now. At the very least, I compare my own gains and losses with how other people appear to be getting along.

I measure out the moments of my life in seconds, minutes, days, and years. Acting as though this objective ordering actually allows accurate evaluation of my existence, I neglect the personal experience of subjective time. But seemingly senseless and unexpected reversals of my wishes repeatedly discredit whatever progressive movement I had in mind. I find that many moments *in* my life are experienced as interruptions *of* my life.

Making the most of life's interruptions and reversals is an overwhelmingly awesome undertaking. What am I to do? When I surrender my sensible self by suspending disbelief in the Hindu Pantheon, then Brahma, Vishnu, and Shiva are available to instruct me in appropriate attitudes of creating, sustaining, and destroying.

It all begins with Brahma . .

BANTAM NEW AGE BOOKS

This important imprint includes books in a variety of fields and disciplines and deals with the search for meaning, growth, and change. They are books that circumscribe our times and our future.

Ask your bookseller for the books you have missed.

HERE I AM, WASN'T I!

The Inevitable Disruption of Easy Times

Sheldon Kopp

BANTAM BOOKS
TORONTO · NEW YORK · LONDON · SYDNEY · AUCKLAND

HERE I AM, WASN'T I!: THE INEVITABLE DISRUPTION OF EASY TIMES

A Bantam Book / February 1986

*New Age and the accompanying figure design as well as
the statement "a search for meaning, growth and change"
are trademarks of Bantam Books, Inc.*

ISBN 0-553-25424-3

Published simultaneously in the United States and Canada

PRINTED IN THE UNITED STATES OF AMERICA

O   0 9 8 7 6 5 4 3 2 1

In appreciation of the rich
second harvest of my marriage,
my grandchildren:
Daren, Stephen, Noah, and Laura.

Contents

Chapter 1

No Nirvana Without Samsara

Whenever I am having fun, time flies. When I am troubled, time drags on so slowly that my discomfort seems as if it will never end. Any attempt to alter the experienced ebb and flow of time automatically exaggerates its pace. When I try to make the good moments last longer, they disappear like the wail of a passing train: Here I am, wasn't I![1] Attempts to speed the passage of the bad moments only serve to slow them down even more.

No matter how I may be feeling at any particular time, objectively I understand that the moment will pass. But simply knowing that nothing lasts does not lessen my inability to turn time's flow to my advantage. Too often I needlessly increase how long I suffer troubled times. I make the most of enjoying easy times less often.

Taking good times too much for granted while insisting that unhappiness is not necessary is foolish. Western culture supports this stubborn shortsightedness. Time is conceived as moving along a straight line on which conditions are certain to improve. The Judeo-Christian religious perspective optimistically evaluates each event as an act of Providence that takes us toward a time when bad things will no longer happen to good people. Secular science promises progress that will advance us all into a technologically utopian society. Contemporary psychological and political consciousness-raising idealize a self so liberated from hangups that one day we will "get it all together" and live in a world free from poverty, prejudice, and war.

In spite of the culture's unkept promises and abetted by personal stubbornness, the quality of my life remains an unpredictable uneven cycle of periods of easy living disrupted by troubled times. Every unexpected change catches me unprepared. Each moment requires its own solution.

I have not always experienced life in this way. As a child of my generation, I was raised on the outdated myths and metaphors of modern Western culture and of a Jewish subculture. To typify the virtues I was taught to believe would be rewarded by Providence and Progress, hardworking Horatio Alger and Honest Abe Lincoln were set side by side with mythic models of the long-suffering chosen children of Israel.

Myths and metaphors shape the adventure of understanding the life we live. But as an adolescent in the 1950s, I crossed a midcentury watershed that marked the burnout of our culture and the flickering fire of the dying embers of its myths and metaphors. Religious belief in Providence could not encompass the Holocaust. The "war to end all wars" had turned out to be only the first in an ongoing series of world conflicts so unstoppable that they had to be designated by Roman numerals. Scientific progress had left us the terrifying legacy of the atomic bomb. The recent political promise of idealist Marxism was wiped away by Stalinism.

Like some other disillusioned and despairing young men and women of my generation, I turned to the contemporary crisis intervention of existentialism. In an heroic attempt to meet the collapse of our anachronistic myths, it individualized each of our lives by telling us that there was no meaning except for the particular story each of us told. At first it was heartening to feel free to choose what my life would mean. Eventually the isolating nihilism of this empty outlook left only a lonely world of "hollow men eating their naked lunches in the Wasteland while awaiting Godot."[2]

Unable to make sense of life without myths to mark its meaning, along with others I gave up going West and turned toward the Orient. Translations of the teachings of Eastern religions had become more available. The easiest escape from the disappointing trap of European existentialism was invited by its Oriental counterpart, Japanese Zen instruction on the absurdity of reason. After a time, Zen ended up as just another empty experiment in mind-fucking. Longing for some feeling-ful sense of community, I made my way to the more humanistic, good-humored playfulness of Chinese Taoism.

Along the way to where I have ended up, I made a long stopover in Indian Buddhism. I did not move on until a Buddhist priest generously helped me to make my way through murky translations of some Sanskrit sutras. He was a little round holy man whose shaven, brown-skinned head topped off a wonderful orange saffron robe, a model of Buddha's sweet acceptance of the universe. Before I left, I talked to him about my grief over my father's death. He said there was no need for sadness because "the world is perfect just as it is."

The remoteness of his detachment was not where I wanted to live my life. Buddhism be damned! The residue of the Western myths on which I was raised has made my quest not one of losing myself but of finding my self.

Despite my disappointment in what Buddhism had to offer, I knew that immersion in Oriental studies had lessened my insistence on taking myself so seriously. Eventually this encouraged my giving up scholarly study of esoteric philosophy and religion for the fun of reading wonder tales of faraway places and long-ago times such as the Indian epics that popularize age-old Hindu myths. These tales altered my understanding of times of change in both my own life and in the lives of my psychotherapy patients.

Viewed from the East, time is a repeated round of births, deaths, and rebirths. I take the concept of reincarnation to be a symbol of the many opportunities for psychological and spiritual rebirth present in each person's life. The broken circle of time is an apt metaphor for my experience of this one and only life we each get to live. The Hindu concept of samsara is the wheel of sorrow to which we are bound by the consequences of bad karma, those accumulated obligations that arise out of ignorance and bad actions in past lives. Nirvana is the release from the suffering of those who give up the illusion that is life. For those of us who go on living, life is a cosmic crap-shoot in which no one stays on a roll.

The Hindu pantheon is made up of the many gods needed to oversee this flux of constancy and change. Each offers an attitude suited to the next segment along the uneven edge of time's broken circle. I must deal differently with life's delights and with its disruptions without ever forgetting that there is *no Nirvana without samsara*, no life without problems, no joy without some sorrow.

Keeping in mind this repeating round of constancy and change serves me well through alternating moments of calm and disruption. It allows me to feel less arrogant when things are going well, and less inadequate when I run into unexpected trouble. But this circular sense of time does more than simply ease my way through daily moment-to-moment shifts from pleasure to pain and back. Without it, and unaided by attitudes inspired by the Hindu deities, I don't know how I would have made it through the second half of my life.

It was this same peculiarly Oriental vision that allowed me to endure a midlife turning so terrible that suicide had seemed my only alternative. Paradoxically, it was this same reorientation that then kept me from missing out on a second, later life turning so wonderful that I was unable at first to imagine it as mine to enjoy.

During the first half of my life, I had established an illusory image of who I thought I was. This earlier sense of self was too one-sided and inflexible not to have been shattered by changes so momentous. I had to identify with appropriate aspects of the Hindu gods Shiva and Vishnu to tolerate the psychological round of death and rebirth evoked by awesomely terrible and sublime subsequent throws of life's dice.

By the time I reached the crisis of my middle life, I had raised children during the time of easy availability of dangerous drugs and the painful madness of the Vietnam war. My family made it through without major casualties. The nest emptied as my sons succeeded in leaving home intact. I became a professionally satisfied psychotherapist while watching many other rewarding careers atrophy into emptiness, boredom, and complacency. Improbably, before I reached forty, phase-appropriate concerns about an empty nest and professional burnout were obscured by the onset of a life-threatening, ultimately incurable illness that would pain me for the remainder of my life.

As of some fifteen years ago, clumsily, but for the most part successfully, I had made my way through most of the usual rites of passage. The culture had provided some of the rituals and agents needed to support me through these painful ordeals. With a little help from loving friends and family, I muddled through on my own. Several times I sought psychotherapy as a patient.

At age thirty-eight, I was a professionally successful psychotherapist, an often happy husband in a lasting marriage, and a proud father of three fascinatingly different sons. The culture supported my denials of the upcoming disruptive passages of illness, aging, and death. Except for contracting for health and life insurance policies, I ignored anticipating that time would require my meeting these awful, inescapable necessities.

As a result, I was helplessly unprepared for the personal catastrophe of suffering a brain tumor that has so far necessitated undergoing three ordeals of neurosurgery, is certain to require other operations in the future, and that eventually will kill me.[3] In retrospect, I realize that I was most overwhelmed by the changed status from physically well young man to chronically ill partial invalid. Gradual adaptation allowed me to overcome the depression that bound me too long to the painful past, to get on with living my life as it is in the present, and to plan for the future by undertaking the partial redemption of past losses with prosthetic compensations for my physical handicaps.

The neurosurgeon offered the first model for the further modifications I later undertook. By the time I underwent the third operation, the tumor had grown so large that it displaced the brainstem sufficiently to shift the pressure buildup of cerebrospinal fluids from one ventricle of the brain to another. This increased my already unbearable head pain and threatened my vision and other as yet unaffected life functions. To correct this menacing problem, the surgeon installed a subdural shunting tube that redirected the fluid from my brain to another part of my body, where it could be innocuously reabsorbed into the vascular system.

At first it seemed intolerable to contemplate even the *idea* of having an alien mechanical device in my body. But as I accepted this "unnatural" presence, I began to imagine other ways in which I might "artificially" ameliorate the destructive changes my body had undergone. Emotionally, the easiest change to consider was having my teeth fixed. A long early history of poor dentistry, teeth broken under deep anesthesia during surgery, and a bite set awry by postsurgical partial facial paralysis had left me with many missing teeth and poorly supporting gums.

Correcting my dental problems seemed emotionally easy only when compared with other losses and disfigurements that more crucially jeopardized who I am and how I make my way in the world. But even the more minimal dental problems made me feel that I had grown old too early and that my body was falling apart. After months of dull, dreary, and uncomfortable encounters with oral surgeons and periodontists, I was delighted to discover that my partial plates not only restored my capacity for eating a wide range of appetizing foods but unexpectedly also helped to correct my facial disfigurement and to improve my partially slurred speech.

Encouraged by the outcome of this prosthetic procedure, I went on to investigate improving the "dry eye" syndrome that so often accompanies acoustic neuroma brain tumors.[4] This condition occurs when the eye no longer blinks reflexively and so does not maintain a smooth protective film of tears over the cornea. It causes blurred, often double vision and engenders an aggravatingly persistent feeling of having something in the eye. This "foreign body" sensation is the result of the drying of the exposed cornea.

Eyedrops, ointment, medicated inserts, and wearing an eyepatch all helped some, but none helped a hell of a lot. I consulted an eye surgeon and arranged to undergo a "minor, in-and-out procedure under a local anesthetic" that lifted my sagging atrophied eyebrow muscle, and sutured my eyelids into a more natural position. All of this eased my ocular discomfort. The improvements were more than I feared and less than I hoped.

This reconstruction allowed me to give up wearing an eyeglass frame equipped with a protective plastic moisture chamber. As a result, I was able to consider getting new glasses that could encase a hearing aid as a hedge against the total deafness in my left ear. In addition to limiting what can be heard, unilateral deafness poses the side effect of creating an auditory blind side, making it difficult to localize where sounds originate. This had long left me confused by the background noises in situations such as at group meetings, in restaurants, at social gatherings, and at public events. I had adjusted to all of this as well as I could, but getting a crossover hearing aid system made it much easier. The CROS has a microphone built into the eyeglass temple on the deaf side. Otherwise unheard sounds are picked up, amplified, and transmitted to the undamaged ear by a microradio transmitter-receiver.

I must admit that being an introverted intuitive psychological type, I was delighted not only with turning up the sound of other people speaking, but with turning it down as well. In large measure, I had adapted to all these handicaps (as well as to the limited mobility that came of symptomatic physical imbalance) by becoming even more sedentary and solitary than before I was ill. With the exception of my devotion to my wife, to a very small number of close personal friends, and to my work as a psychotherapist, I had withdrawn increasingly into an inner vision soothed by the cherished solitude of reading and writing books and nourished by the recorded sounds of jazz, blues, and baroque music. My situation would have been much more difficult had I been an extrovert engaged in encountering the outside world, a feeling type attached to the unavailable past, or a sensation type attracted to adventures in the present.

Though I often missed my kids, their growing up and leaving home simplified my situation even more. For a while, I was back in the easy constancy of unchanging time. My wife and I had discovered what it was like each having individual lives of our own. At the same time we found new ways to be together as we adapted creatively to her building a postchild-rearing career and to my own house-husbanding while coping with chronic illness. At times it was as confused and painful as we could make it, but often it was sounder and sweeter than I could have imagined such radical reorientations to be.

The recently renewed circle of easy constant times was soon to be unexpectedly broken once again. The promise of the empty nest was broken by my grown children returning either in person, or in our concern for their changing situations. As each son returned he brought with him a woman, with or without a child. It was clear that we had not lost our sons. Not only had we gained daughters, but a grandchild as well. I now believe that we had unconsciously assigned each son the task of finding an interesting woman who had missed out on having a satisfactory family of her own. These

newfound daughters could then be brought back home
to become part of our own family.

During this return of my sons and their retinue, I
offered emotional support, financial subsidy, attention
redirected from my own introverted fortress, and personal services that drained energy and stamina already
limited by illness. I tried to give all of this openly,
lovingly, and graciously, but often my internal irritation
was obvious.

Focusing my complaints on the kids' invasions of my
private space, as well as on how heavily my illness
weighed as I trudged from one end of the day to the
other, I spoke of them privately to my wife and friends.
Rather than dump these matters directly on my sons, it
was my intention to sort through my feelings carefully,
to clarify the order of my emotional priorities, and to
adjust my actions responsibly to fit both taking care of
myself and showing my devotion to my family. To my
surprise, during these conversations I gradually began
to realize that I was expressing more pleasure than
distress.

I was made aware of the impact and of the opportunities offered by this latest break in the constancy of my
life first by a series of changed experiences and then by
instruction rendered by recalling a dream dreamed during the disruption. At the time of all this restoration and
expansion of the family, the entrance/exit to our home
had begun to seem like a revolving door.

I awoke one Monday to the comfortingly familiar ease
of my regular morning routines. The clock radio turned
on to wake me with everyday early-morning jazz on the
black community radio station. As always, it was soft
and mellow as I woke from the privacy of sleep to be
ushered into what I usually fear will be a too-public
day. As usual, my wife was already off to work. At first

I resented this separation, but I had come to accept the period of grace it granted me. It offered a chance for me to reintegrate my sleep-shattered self with my introverted personality so that both of us could contend with all the other people in my day.

Assuring me of the adaptations I had made to illness, putting in place the denture plates and hearing aid felt like fitting myself out for whatever the day might bring. Reading those sections of *The Washington Post* that I peruse each morning over solitary breakfast and cigar felt fine. Driving almost automatically over my regular route through the park to my office allowed uninterrupted anticipation of the day's scheduled appointments for psychotherapy and supervision, unmarred by external distraction of traffic or other external events.

The following morning should have paralleled Monday's peace. Instead, Tuesday broke like a watershed abruptly shifting one stage of my life to the next. The clock radio's early-morning mellow jazz no longer seemed lively enough to accompany my march from darkness into the bright light of day. Uneasy with my wife's early exit from bedroom to boardroom, I felt disappointed that my returned prodigal son was not awake so that we could talk over breakfast. The morning's routines made the time drag, and I experienced the insertions of denture plates and hearing aid as assaults by inanimate objects. I drove to my office by a road less traveled while wondering whether I was starting to get stuck in work habits that would bring me to a burnout.

Later, remembering how differently I had experienced the same events from one day to the next, I felt certain that I had misplaced a dream dreamed during the night between those two mismatched mornings. Then it came to me. I remembered dreaming of a visit to a remarkable house.

Bit by bit, fragments of that dream floated to the surface of my daytime consciousness. Slowly the pieces reassembled into clear, coherent recollection. Most of my dreams involve seeing myself alone in some sparse symbolic setting, eventually encountering one other often anonymous creature. This time I was astonishingly aware of extravagantly detailed surroundings and of a complex cast of characters. Even more startling was my ending up comfortably committed to remaining in the dream-setting instead of my more usual resolution of heroically heading off beyond its boundaries.

As the recalled dream begins, my wife and I are entering a magnificent mansion that is the newly opened home of her closest friend. I understand that this is the "dream house" the friend has always wanted. The occasion of our visit is a housewarming party of the sort that my waking self would never even consider attending.

The house is extravagantly large, lavishly furnished, and filled with colorfully dressed visitors actively socializing with each other while luxuriantly partaking of elegantly catered gourmet offerings. I am aware of a vague response of revulsion to what seems too gaudy and demanding an array of sensory bombardment. Paradoxically, at the same time I feel drawn toward losing myself in the festivities.

The husband of the hostess is a stereotypically bohemian Greenwich Village artist. Taking me by the arm, he leads me around the first floor of the house to see his paintings. They seem to fill every available inch of wall space. I find his works superficial and lacking in creative commitment. Arrogantly I assert that though they may qualify as decoration certainly they are not art.

Uncharacteristically, I bear with his seeming self-indulgence, letting him lead me up the spiral staircase to the second floor. On this next level, I am awed both by visual access to a vast outdoor deck spectacularly over-looking the ocean and by how much warmer and hom-ier this part of the house feels to me.

Up here, the painter's productions impress me with the rich beauty of their intense earthy colors. These paintings show compelling commitment. They are amaz-ingly unlike the others I encountered on entering the house. I say to myself, "Now, this is art you can live with!"

Up to this point, I have been uncomfortable amid the social chatter of the other gallery-opening drop-ins. Now, as I listen less self-consciously, I discover that the other guests have many interesting things to say. Spending time with them turns out to be surprisingly satisfying.

All at once, I discover that I have taken off all my clothes. My nudity feels fine. I learn that we are all to join in some further festivity. My clothes are piled on a chair. I decide to wear only my jeans. Bare-footed and bare-chested, I feel freer and more at home than at any party I have ever attended. My disturbingly transitional dream has ended up offering unexpectedly promising possibilities.

The wheel of time continues its erratic turning through its periodically broken circle. The changes that inter-rupt the ease of comfortable constancy are inevitably upsetting, but embedded in their disruption are opportu-nities offered for the challenge of coping with new necessities. Fresh awareness of lived time replaces the unconscious passing of stale time. The current disrup-tive necessity requires my surrender to emergence out of isolated introversion and immersion into full family living. Finding a way to live with the contradictions will again demand the evoking of all my emotional resources.

Otherwise I risk betrayal either of my private self or of the people I love most.

Seeing my sons through completion of their educations, establishment of their careers, and recovery from misadventures, I must try not to meddle as I offer support to their mating, marrying, and making families of their own. More and more this seems exactly the experience to which I will devote this time of my life.

One son brought home not only a lovely young woman to marry, but her child from a previous relationship as well. During these many years of illness, I was afraid that I would die before having a grandchild. As soon as this baby unexpectedly entered my life, I fell in love with him.

The women my sons have brought home are all survivors of hard times. They are very different from one another, and I relate very differently to each of them. Still, they all have in common an intriguing amalgam of toughness and vulnerability that is the vibrant legacy of people who somehow have managed to survive suffering, neglect, and abuse while all the while still hungering for the good life. Recent breaks in the circle of this time of my own life have sometimes seemed so disruptively harsh that for a while I experienced a loss of appetite for life. But into emotional areas opened up by those disruptions, this grandchild and these newfound daughters have entered to restore my enthusiasm for this next experience of easy living.

NOTES

1. Lawrence LeShan, *How to Meditate: A Guide to Self-Discovery*, with an Afterword by Edgar N. Jackson (New York: Bantam Books, 1975), p. 55. Among people who practice Yoga, this popular adage is known as "The Law of the Good Moment."

2. Robert Nisbet, *History of the Idea of Progress* (New York: Basic Books, 1980), p. 328.

3. I have written elsewhere in detail about other aspects of this experience. The most recent detailed account appears in my last book, *The Pickpocket and the Saint: The Free Play of Imagination* (New York: Bantam Books, 1983).

4. In this and other attempts to understand, adapt to, and improve my situation, I was helpfully informed by *Acoustic Neuroma Association Notes*, a patient-oriented newsletter published by the Acoustic Neuroma Association, P.O. Box 398, Carlisle, PA 17013.

Chapter 2

It's About Time

In these life crises, both the problems and their solutions were strongly subject to my changing sense of time. We tend to take time for granted as a straightforward, obvious aspect of physical reality. When desperate circumstances call closer attention to its passing, time turns out to be more mercurial. As the mythologist Joseph Campbell writes: "What is time? When you do not ask me, I know; but when you ask me, I no longer know."[1] The unexamined concept of time is very different from its experienced passage in our personal lives.

When I think about time, I imagine it passing in a predictable and orderly sequence of objective, consistent segments. My experience of time, however, is strikingly different from my idea of what time is like. I may think of time as an unchanging flow of measured minutes, but the events of my life occur in a subjective unwinding of elastic experience that sometimes speeds up and seems to fly and sometimes slows down and drags on.

Everything that happens occurs at a particular point *in* time, but always the subjective meaning of each event depends in part on the context of what I remember having happened just before it and what I expect will happen next. An isolated event can be charted as having occurred on a particular date at a specific time of day. I live in the present moment, but my sense of the present is framed by memories of the past and expectations of the future.

Whatever I experience as "now" continually changes as I move through the ongoing passage of its relative place in the unstoppable movement of my conception of past, present, and future. Paradoxically, within that shifting sequence, whatever occurred earlier than or later than a particular event remains firmly in place, even as the last "now" so quickly becomes the next "then." And yet each moment adds to the orderly auto-biography I perceive to be my personal history.

Like the measurable minutes, hours, days, months, and years, my sense of before and after remains independent of the ever-changing place of "now" in time passing. Like my sense of self, my experience of time is both constant and changing. How am I to reconcile these contradictions of permanence and change?

Duration is the normal experience of time passing. The indifferent intervals of clock time are unresponsive to personal need. Even so, objective ideas of time seem so real that often I struggle desperately "to make time" and "not to waste time." Like those midwestern American farmers who recently opposed daylight saving time "because they felt that the extra hour of sunlight would burn the grass,"[2] I, too, confuse clock and calendar time with human time.

Some psychologists[3] have suggested that the elasticity of the experience of lived time depends on how much information we process in any given period of clock time. Obviously, the amount of stimuli with which any person must deal varies. But the more changes we experience, the more time seems to speed up; the fewer the changes, the more it seems to slow down.

Both situations may be experienced as either positive or negative. At best, for a self that is safe and secure, the seemingly simple state of constancy brings with it the calm of familiar times that are slow and easy. In its negative aspect, the sameness of repeated routines can become boring, and the self ends up feeling stuck.

When changes are rapid and radical, I may delight in a "time [that] passes so quickly when you're having fun." In times of crisis, these same changes can feel distressingly disruptive. In that crunch, unable to enjoy the novelty of unfamiliar occurrences, I may feel overstimulated, overwhelmed, or even victimized. Suddenly everything seems to be happening at once.

The complexity of the contrasts is clearest when I leave a familiar situation for a chosen change and later return. For example, after a long segment of regularly scheduled office work, I may choose a brief but dramatically different vacation setting. When it's time to return, there is a feeling of having been away for a long time. But back in the office once again, suddenly the vacation no longer seems so long. When I am able to reconcile these contradictions, I integrate the vacation changes into renewal of the work energy. Otherwise the discontinuity makes the resumed work even more routinized than it seemed before the trip.

In addition to the impact of situational changes, the ways in which the experience of time varies for any given person is colored by the contrasting perceptions of different cultures and social classes. When members of one culture encounter another, these group differences range from superficial conflicts about punctuality and deadlines to varying time perspectives almost unimaginable from one group to another.

Some cultures still deeply embedded in tribal or mythic visions of existence discriminate between the measurable, ordinary, ongoing time of daily life and the sacred ceremonial timelessness of ritual occasions. Some live most of life in a time incongruent with the contemporary American/European time continuum.[4]

In the language of the Hopi Indians, for instance, life in the eternal present is reflected by an absence of past, present, and future verb tenses. Hopi temporal concepts such as winter and summer are not nouns. The seasons are experienced as adverbial conditions during which the group prepares for sacred ceremonies. Ritual transitions are unmarked by the clear-cut divisions of American/European time categories. At my wedding, one minute I was an unattached bachelor without family responsibilities. A moment later, I was a married man committed for life to one woman and to the children we would bear. Had I been a Hopi warrior, my marriage would have included more than two dozen different events spaced out over an entire year.

Cultures like our own are dominated by traditionally male, task-oriented, beginning-middle-end linear approaches directed toward accomplishment. Some other cultures experience time as rotating in a traditionally female, people-oriented circle. They experience time as defined by interpersonal relationships rather than by work schedules. Our culture values time in terms of its being full and productive. The relationship-oriented culture puts human needs and matters of the heart ahead of progress and "logical" considerations.

Situational shifts change the experience of time during the life of any one person. Cultural conditions contribute to differences of temporal perspective between groups. Individual personality and style influence how people within the same group characteristically experience their lived time. Experiences of constancy and change as well as of past, present, and future differ radically from one psychological temperament to another.

Understanding how time is experienced requires consideration of the contribution of individual temperament. However, any attempt to understand how personality type influences time perspectives is undertaken at the risk of ignoring the unique outlook of any particular person. Attempts to categorize human beings into personality types may put people into dehumanizing pigeonholes. Even so, in our struggle to bring manageable order to the overwhelming chaos that is life, we all classify our experience of objects, events, and creatures into recognizable, partially predictable groupings.

Like everyone else, I judge other people. I am less interested in figuring out if my judgments are "true" or "false" than I am in understanding whether they seem helpful. When I practice psychotherapy, thinking of people as being of one sort or another is often useful in helping them to be happier. Despite the risk of dehumanizing categorization, personal rigidity, and downright foolishness, I often use the concepts of psychological types as guidelines.

Every such system of sorting souls is arbitrary and flawed. Each judgment is subjective and may turn out to be simply incorrect. When the judgments I make lead to impasses in therapy, I try to revise or to set them aside if they interfere with my getting to know a patient better.

Compared with classifying people by psychodiagnostic titles of mental health and mental illness, categorizing people into a system of psychological types is relatively free of ennobling and pejorative valuations. Even so, though all of the many scientific, astrological, literary, aesthetic, and philosophical systems for categorizing human beings according to behavior, attitude, and personality[5] sometimes turn out to be useful, often they can be misleading, and ultimately are all fanciful. In attempting to understand people's characteristic personality styles, categorizing by Jungian psychological types[6] seems to me as good a system and as bad a set of metaphors as many of the other imaginative classifications.

Using a psychological type theory of personality offers several advantages. Otherwise, overwhelmed by life's seemingly endless variety of differences among people, I *must* generalize to begin to understand. The categories chosen need to reflect basic human characteristics existing in all individuals in differing proportions. The vivid extremes of these idealizations can then serve as guideposts for the variations encountered in particular people. For my purposes, use of psychological types works better than most judgments in honoring the uniqueness of each individual and in avoiding positive or negative valuing of one type over another.

Despite the danger of reducing living beings to abstract ideals, keeping in mind that they may have different basic personality styles makes me less likely to ask people to live in some way that is not their own. Many painful psychological problems can be alleviated by self-acceptance based on recognition of who we are. In the same way, many interpersonal conflicts can be resolved by reciprocal appreciation of the conflicting and fundamental differences in perspective between people of potentially complementary outlooks. Neither need be judged as neurotic or healthy, mature or immature, right or wrong.

The evaluative question in the use of psychological type theory is not "What type am I?" but rather "How good am I at being myself?" Secretly I know that however hard I may try to accept the style of others as equivalent to my own, too often I find myself either envious of someone else's "better" style, or patronizingly self-satisfied that my way is preferable. At such times I need only remember that like the gods themselves, each personality style works better in some situations and worse in others.

Keeping all of those advantages and cautions in mind, Jung's psychological types can be useful in understanding how people may experience time differently. For Jung, the most basic difference in personalities is the tendency toward extroversion or introversion. This dichotomy serves as a helpful distinction about the direction of people's attitudes toward self and toward the world.[7] However, it is less crucial to the individual's sense of time than are the four modes of experiencing life described by Jung: thinking, feeling, sensation, and intuition.[8]

Thinking types depend primarily on ideas and logic to make sense of experience. For such people, time is a linear stream measurably flowing in an orderly progression from the past through the present to the future. Their rational detachment allows a long-range overview from which they may assess cause and effect. They believe that this cognitive distancing allows them the advantage of living according to rational principles, accurate predictions, and sensible plans.

At best, thinking types are well-organized, long-range planners who make careful decisions that others may act upon. At their worst, people who attempt to transcend the necessities of the moment logically can be rigid, unfeeling, narrow-minded, and dogmatic, readily sacrificing emotions for explanations. In their attempts to be beyond time, thinking types are acutely unprepared for crises and may miss out on the immediate experience of their own personal place in time's irrational flow.

Feeling types are their polar counterparts. Nostalgically embedded in emotions tied to their own personal pasts, such people are uncomfortable in new impersonal or unrelated situations. The only current events that interest them are those emotionally intense enough to become something to remember. For feeling types, time is an eternal return in which the meaning of the present and the future depend entirely on their promise of restoring a glorious past or compensating for a disappointing personal history.

At their best, feeling types live warm, colorful lives, loyally committed to emotionally rich relationships. At their worst, with experience embedded in time past, they insist that everything remain the same. This leaves these people vulnerable to exaggerated unhappiness when they meet the unexpected changes, inevitable losses, and unavoidable disappointments of time's indifference to their longings.

Jung's perpendicular polar axis to the thinking/feeling functions is the intersection of sensation/intuition psychological types. The detached overview of the thinking type is directed toward explaining *why* life goes on as it does, *past, present, and future*. The nostalgically emotional investment of the feeling type is focused on *how it feels* in relation to the *past*. The more practical perspective of the sensation type reacts exclusively to *what* is happening in the *present*, while the intuitive type's fascination with mystery makes much of *what it all means* for the *future*.

Concretely discriminating between what is and what is not directly given to the senses, the sensation type is completely committed to the hard facts of occurrences in the present. Adventuresome at their best, they are tough-mindedly effective in emergencies and calm in crises. At worst, the price of this practicality is the impatient urge to undertake immediate action. Living as they do in the immediate present, sensation types forego the complexity of time enriched by inferences out of the past and given purpose by implications for the future.

Intuitive types like myself tend to ignore what is going on right now and how it came about except as we imagine past and present implying meaning for the future. Our attention is on the horizon, whether it be the utopia or apocalypse of the extroverted intuitive or the deepening inner vision of introverts like myself. At our best, we find life filled with meaning that inspires us with envisioned implications of each moment. Even when we are right, we risk forcing meaning out of each unconnected moment. Though we are always certain about the future, we are often wrong about what we imagine it to be. At our worst we may miss out on what we might have gleaned from the past, sown in the present, and harvested in a future better anchored in its antecedents.

Just as culturally determined perspectives make for differing experiences of time from one group to another, within each group, psychological types contribute to differences in individual temporal outlooks. Nonetheless, there are timebound transitions with which everyone must contend. Developmental crises such as the child's growth into adolescence and then into adulthood, courtship, and marriage; the establishing of a social identity; illness, aging, and death are common fare for everyone.

All societies provide some ceremonial rites of passage[9] for supporting individual members during the separations and reincorporations needed to make their way through these disruptive necessities of lived time. At that break in the circle of time when each person enters a status at variance with the one previously held, he or she steps out of history and into nature. Primitive groups offer a ceremonial cushion to ease the disturbing passage through changes from profane to sacred time. Because of their more secular, rational, individualistic outlooks, contemporary Western societies are less likely than tribal cultures to help people through the turmoil that surrounds these common crises. The psychotherapist has become the Western agent for helping unsupported individuals who fail to find satisfying resolutions for getting through these crises on their own.

Psychotherapy patients often have not successfully completed some crucial passages from one stage of life to the next. The interruption of calm and constancy accompanying each change left the individual in limbo, temporarily alienated and unclaimed until, with or without outside help, the incompatibility of the old and the new statuses can be resolved.

Like territorial passages in space, developmental passages in time are marked by milestones and boundary posts. Each crossroad or portal is a point of passage that is physically, psychologically, or spiritually dangerous. Offerings, invocations, or sacrifices to the gods must be made to ensure safe passage. Among highly ritualized Orthodox Jews, every change must be blessed if it is not to be cursed. Each time the threshold of the main door of the house is crossed, the Jew must touch a finger of the right hand to the *mezuzah*. Attached to the doorpost, this ritual ornament contains a ribbon on which is embroidered the sacred name of God. Kissing the sanctified finger, the Jew intones, "The Lord shall preserve thy going out and thy coming in from this time forth evermore."

NOTES

1. From the Editor's Foreword in *Man and Time: Papers from the Eranos Yearbooks*, ed. Joseph Campbell, Bollingen Series XXX—3 (Princeton, N.J.: Princeton University Press, 1983), p. xi.

2. Robert E. Ornstein, *On the Experience of Time* (New York: Penguin Books, 1975), p. 27.

3. Ibid.

4. Edward T. Hall, *The Dance of Life: The Other Dimension of Time* (Garden City, N.Y.: Anchor Press/Doubleday & Company, 1983).

5. Ralph Metzner, *Know Your Type: Maps of Identity* (Garden City, N.Y.: Anchor Press/Doubleday & Company, 1979).

6. C.G. Jung, "Psychological Types," in *The Collected Works of C.G. Jung, Volume 6*, a revision by R.S.C. Hull of the translation by H.G. Baynes, Bollingen Series II (Princeton, N.J.: Princeton University Press, 1971).

7. Sheldon Kopp, *The Hanged Man: Psychotherapy and the Forces of Darkness* (Palo Alto, Calif.: Science and Behavior Books, 1974). For a more detailed analysis of Jung's psychological types, see Chapter 7, "The Karma of Personality," pp. 105–26.

8. Harriet Mann, Miriam Siegler, and Humphrey Osmond, "Four Types of Personalities and Four Ways of Perceiving Time," *Psychology Today*, Vol. 6, No. 7 (December 1972), pp. 76ff. From the book *The Future of Time*, ed. Humphrey Osmond, Henri Yaker, and Frances Cheek (Garden City, N.Y.: Doubleday & Company, 1971).

9. Arnold van Gennep, *The Rites of Passage*, trans. Monika B. Vizedom and Gabrielle L. Caffee (Chicago: University of Chicago Press, 1960).

Chapter 3

Changing of the Gods

Hindu cosmology provides a metaphor of time as a broken circle. Hindu mythology is a guide for taking a turn on that wheel of joy and sorrow. Tales of contrasting and complementary aspects of its many gods serve as models for the changing attitudes appropriate to cycles of easy living, inevitable interruption, and eventual resumption. This configuration has helped me to stop squandering my appetite on the bitter aftertaste of sorrow so I may savor joy more slowly.

The linear Western model of time fits the abstract ideals to which I was taught to aspire. The circular Oriental conception is more congruent with the unending ups and downs of human experience. Relentless and repeated cycles of creation, preservation, and destruction of the broken cosmic circle capture more clearly life's continuing contrasts of constancy and change. Each cycle of divine day and night in the life of the Hindu gods encompasses thousands of human years. Every great rotating cycle is an inevitable and repeated sequence of the four world ages. In each cycle the universe is created in perfect order, only to fall into renewed disorder. Ultimately all is destroyed until the time of the next round of re-creation.

The four ages of each cycle are called *yugas*. Each is named after a throw of the dice in the cosmic game of life. The new beginning of the Krita Yuga comes up as a four that wins the jackpot. In perfect order, the newly created universe is squarely set on all of its four legs. It is a sweet, dependable time of easy living. Everything seems to go right in a world in which life makes sense.

But following each firmly founded, four-footed first age, the Treta Yuga of the second throw of the dice tenaciously turns up a three. The spontaneously sound order of life begins to lapse into decay. Standing on only three of its four legs, preserving a solid balance now needs work. It's harder to be loving when you're losing. Kindness now calls for conscious effort. Duty and devotion no longer come naturally. If doing right is not to deteriorate into self-indulgent irresponsibility, deliberate self-discipline is demanded. Only because we believe that things will have to get better can we keep on trying.

The next throw of the dice is a two. Instead of getting better in the Dvapara Yuga, life gets worse. Tottering on two legs, the uneasy balance of order and disorder becomes increasingly unstable. Self-confidence and high ideals give way to panicky, mean-spirited grabbing for whatever we can get. We insist that soon conditions will improve. In the meantime, until life gets back to normal, we might as well make the best of a bad situation.

Paradoxically, our opportunistic struggle to survive this disruption ushers in the subsequent still darker age of the Kali Yuga. The fourth throw of the dice is always a one. We lose it all. This Hindu equivalent of snake eyes brings about the absolute awfulness of everything. The blind necessity of disorder invites total degradation. Responding recklessly, we are all at our worst. For a time life seemed so sweet and secure. Now there is no escaping its total disruption.

These four ages of humankind have taken place during a single day in the life of the original creator, Brahma. And now, during an equivalent time of divine night, while the creator sleeps, human life is left in limbo and the universe in ruins.

The creation, the rise and the descent of all that exists for mortals, has lasted only one waking day for the gods. The night of dissolution that follows is equal in time. At divine daybreak again the god will awaken to close the broken circle with another first throw of the dice.

People enjoy good times and suffer bad times. For the gods, every age is self-sufficient. Each is necessary. None is judged to be better or worse than any other.

During these millions of good years and bad years, humankind has come and gone. All that seemed so dependable has been lost once again. During disruptions as difficult as these, we can barely imagine that things will ever again return to normal. But for the gods, the making, the breaking, and the remaking of time's circle of illusion involve an inevitable eternal return.

The roll we are on right now will run all of its relentlessly necessary reversals and resumptions. All the alternations in our individually dreamed human lifetimes are indifferent throws of the dice. They last no longer and matter no more than an instant in the life of the gods.

Brahma, the Creator, makes his winning pass in the first yuga. Vishnu, the Sustainer, tries to retain the winnings and to recoup the losses that begin in the second yuga and grow worse in the third. With the fourth throw of the dice, it becomes clear that all will be lost. That night Shiva, the Destroyer, breaks up the crap-shoot so that at dawn of the next divine day Brahma can begin the game again.

The macrocosm of humankind's eras of development and decline is paralleled in miniature by the ephemeral instances of delight and trouble that make up the day-to-day living of individual men and women. Both the sustaining experiences of easy living and their inevitable interruption by hard times occur in all our lives. More and more, it seems to me that these changes, the diversity of the people with whom we wend our way, and even the complexity of each individual personality are all too complex to be sustained sufficiently by a single unified Western vision of life.

We all seem to need the extended ease of those phases of life when we can count on knowing exactly who we are while we settle into a world we appear to understand. When things seem the same we feel safe, but after a while experience grows stale. Our responsiveness to the world about us weakens into sentimentality or is inverted into cynicism. The power of our passion narrows into the dogma of strong opinion until all that's left is approving of some things and disapproving of others. If we are to realize the richness, color, depth, and intensity of experience available to each of us, we must learn to tolerate the discontinuity of life's inevitable episodic interruptions. The return of constancy requires tolerance of change.

An exorbitant emotional price is paid for a forced illusion of consistency. I tell myself that there must be some reasonable way to get beyond the inescapable anxieties and sufferings meted out by lawless chance. If only I were wise enough, I would make no mistakes. If I were somehow good enough, I would be safe from misfortunes. If someone else would only take good enough care of me, then I could be protected from upsetting experiences.

Paradoxically, these short-term illusory assurances leave me chronically unprepared for the inevitable upsets that periodically occur. Insisting on coherence and consistency, I foolishly set myself against changing times. Wishing for a life uninterrupted by random mishaps and personal hang-ups only makes matters worse. My attempt to overcome all adversity is an empty assault against necessity, a fight that no one can win.

Imposing the appearance of order on my life cannot be accomplished without sacrificing freedom, adventure, and surprise. This imposed illusion of control is a deceptive and ineffectual effort to take charge of my life. Ignoring the disorder that is, I miss out on opportunities offered by that very disorder.

Too often I am tempted to believe that my life is an orderly process that means something and is headed somewhere. It seems as though I should be able to tell whether I am making progress. I pace myself against some ideal of how far I should have come by now. At the very least, I compare my own gains and losses with how other people appear to be getting along.

I measure out the moments of my life in standard-size seconds, minutes, days, weeks, months, and years. Acting as though this objective ordering actually allows accurate evaluation of my existence, I neglect the personal experience of subjective time. Whether awed by how much of my life is ahead of me, or astonished at how much is already over, I imagine that I can stem the tide of time, hurry it up, or slow it down. I hope to be able to accomplish more than can be done, or fear that I am wasting time or doing nothing.

But necessity cannot be avoided. Seemingly senseless

and unexpected reversals of my wishes repeatedly discredit whatever progressive movement I might have in mind. If I do not attend to how haphazard happenings turn me this way and that, upside down and inside out, I find that many moments *in* my life are experienced as interruptions *of* my life.

It is difficult to accept comfortably the absence of *some* sustaining segments of order, some hope of stemming suffering and attaining an improved state of being. But the search for happiness cannot be carried out in any simple step-by-step upward ascent.

Deliberate or not, disruptions do occur, and making the most of life's interruptions and reversals is an overwhelmingly awesome undertaking. But trying to bypass those obstacles and alternations often leaves me chronically complaining about how helplessly stuck I feel. What am I to do? When I surrender my sensible self by suspending disbelief in the Hindu pantheon, then Brahma, Vishnu, and Shiva are available to instruct me in appropriate attitudes of creating, sustaining, and destroying.

It all begins with Brahma. Except for my acknowledgment that he is not just this nor only that, Brahma defies definition. He creates the appearances that I experience as life. The world consists only of illusions generated by his playing a cosmic game of hide-and-seek with himself. The endless alternation of experience of self and others, world and void, good and bad, here and there, then and now, are all no more than Brahma revealing and concealing himself.

Unlike Jehovah, Brahma does not construct a universe out of chaos. Instead he creates it by making a multiplicity of alternation and illusion out of division and disruption of the unity of his own identity.

Like all the other Hindu gods, his myths are many.[1]

All offer contradictions beyond consistent resolution, and variations too valuable to risk reduction by synthesis. Even so, if only because of their repetition, some themes seem more central than others. Some others stand out on the strength of their unique singularity. Throughout this book I have chosen those particular mythic variations that move me most. Other tales might suit you better.

All of the Hindu myths celebrate the belief that the universe "is boundlessly various, that everything occurs simultaneously, that all possibilities exist without excluding each other."[2] Because of this polytheistic paradox, the *Upanishad*[3] myth of the creation of the universe by Brahma is very different from the monotheistic, logical, and linear tale of Genesis. According to Western mythic imagination, in the beginning was the Word of the one and only God, Jehovah. Out of the chaos of the void, His Word created the order of the universe.

In one of the Hindu myths of origin, that time before time is only one more turning of the ever-evolving cycles of creation, preservation, and destruction of the illusions known to humans as life in the universe. This particular creation just happens to take place during another one of those disruptions where nothing exists except in the form of Brahma. It is the division and dismemberment of his own existence that generates the ephemeral appearances that we experience as self, others, and the world. On uncountable earlier occasions, it had all happened before. It will all go on happening, constantly changing, time and time again forever.

At different points along the circumference of this broken circle of continuous change, other gods appear to dominate the making and unmaking of it all. During the particular round when all existence is Brahma, the divine original person is alone. Looking around and seeing only himself, the first thing he says is "I am." Out of his creating this identity, we receive the legacy of the illusion that we have a self.

Seeing that he is alone, Brahma is afraid. Because of that, we each imagine that our security in the world depends on being with other people.

In his own moment of desire for company, seeing that he is large enough to be more than one, Brahma splits himself into two pieces. These halves become a husband and a wife. From that splitting we have come to experience our individual self as if it were incomplete in the absence of a love relationship with another.

Brahma fills his empty space with his wife. They make love. That is how there came to be people in the world.

When she realizes that she had once been part of the husband who now makes love to her, the wife feels ashamed. Trying to escape his embrace, she transforms herself into a cow. Brahma turns into a bull. Again he makes love to her. Then there are cattle in the world. Next she tries becoming a mare, but he becomes a stallion. And when she becomes a female ass, Brahma becomes a male ass. Both times again he makes love to her. From those unions, solid-hooved animals are born into the universe.

When she becomes a nanny goat, Brahma becomes a billy goat. And when she becomes a ewe, he becomes a ram. In each transformation, they make love. Since that time there have been goats and sheep. In just this way, Brahma creates all the living things, in whatever pairs there are, from elephants to ants.

Brahma, the original male/female soul, creates by disrupting. His pure consciousness allows him to do this, but it does not allow him to fool himself, as in my own limited awareness I fool myself. He is unable *not* to

know that: "I, indeed, am this creation, for I emitted it
all from myself." Unsettling the peaceful constancy of
sustained ongoing aloneness that is already everything,
he brings forth the fragmentation into the illusion that I
experience as the real world.

I, too, must remember that creation can come only
through change. Whenever I do, I am more easily able
to accept the opportunities for re-creation offered by the
inevitable interruptions I encounter. These disruptions
do not destroy anything of importance. Such changes
merely challenge the constancy of imagined order in the
illusion I experience as my life.

As I come round time's broken circle, I must respond
in turn to each changing of the gods. Each god and
goddess has a style of his or her own suited to particular
situations encountered along its shifting circumference.
Oriental worshipers evoke the needed mental state provided by a given god's characteristic by immersing themselves in meditation and ceremonial ritual. Secular
Westerners can call forth comparable emotional attitudes by rereading the myths and legends, amplifying
each god's offering by introspection, fantasy, guided
imagery, and focused dreaming.

Active imagination is the Occidental equivalent of
Oriental spiritual practices. It is not necessary to be a
Hindu to experience the unity of times that seem divided,
the unity that allows our understanding that there is no
Nirvana without samsara, no joy without some sorrow.

The oneness of it all is illumined by recognition of
the universal soul of Brahma. Honoring Shiva offers
opportunities during periods of disruption. In the face
of growing unexpected losses, Vishnu lovingly sustains
episodes of easy living. I must face each god in sweet
surrender at that segment of time's circle at which his or
her particular cosmic aspect is in ascendance.

NOTES

1. The myths appear in changing variations through-
      out the early Hindu writings: the Vedas
      (1200–900 B.C.), the Upanishads (700 B.C.),
      the Mahabharata and Ramayana epics (300
      B.C.–A.D. 300), the early Puranas (300
      B.C.–A.D. 500), the middle Puranas (A.D.
      500–1000), and the late Puranas (A.D. 1000
      –1500).

2. *Hindu Myths: A Sourcebook Translated from the Sanskrit*
      (Baltimore: Penguin Books, 1975), p. 11.

3. *The Thirteen Principal Upanishads*, trans. from the San-
      skrit (London: Oxford University Press,
      1934), p. 81.

Chapter 4

Honoring Shiva

As my life unwinds along the broken circle of time, again and again I become aware of having experienced cycles of creation, preservation, and disruption. In retrospect, the major mode of most of the first half of my life might metaphorically best be described as disruptive. Cast in the iconography of the diverse divinities of the Hindu pantheon, it is easy to identify the bulk of experienced time in both my personal and professional adult life as the unconscious honoring of Shiva.

His unconventional appearance is an awesome array of brown skin color, a black belly, and a throat stained blue with the residue of poison he swallowed to save the people of the earth. Shiva's appearance made him unwelcome among ordinary people. I, too, have long endured an awkwardly uninviting self-sustained image of the menacing misfit. Clumsily destructive, socially inappropriate, and always seeming to say the wrong thing at the wrong time, for most of my lifetime I have seen my adult self as the gross animal that my mother so often saw me to be when I was a child. Unfit for human company and unacceptable anywhere outside of the family, I thought of myself as a troublemaker whose manner and appearance were certain to offend anyone I met.

Early on, with a vengeance, I gave up trying to be nice. Positive that I could not please, instead I indulged myself in making the most of the menace I imagined myself to be. If it was not my place to please others, I would get my way by intimidating them. If I could not expect to be treated well because I was lovable, I settled for currying not being treated badly by threatening obnoxious retaliation. Master of the insulting one-liner, I was willing to wound anyone who dared to challenge my warrior posture. Effectively argumentative, I fought to the death to protect my right to be openly obscene. Rather than risk being ignored, I chose to be hated. Moralistically inflating an illusory ego ideal of untamed integrity, I carried out my bullying in the china shop of other people's vulnerability and sensitivity.

When he went into the woods to visit the ten thousand sages he deemed heretics, Shiva, too, rode a bull. His intention was to teach them the truth. Because they did not recognize this disheveled ascetic whose skin was covered with dirt and whose matted hair entwined twigs and thorns, they received him with curses. Their spells and condemnations having no effect upon him, they called up a terrible tiger to devour him. Smiling, Shiva took the skin off the tiger with the nail of his little finger and wrapped it around himself like a shawl. When the heretics brought forth a horrible snake, Shiva hung it around his neck like a garland.

The sages turned out a terrible black demon dwarf armed with a mace. Shiva put his foot on the dwarf's back and danced him into the dust. At last the hermits gave up. The heavens opened, the awed gods assembled and faced the dancer with appreciation. Recognizing the disheveled yogin as Shiva himself, the sages fell at his feet to worship him.

Justifying my own obnoxious impact as the equivalent of Shiva's terrible benevolence, I chopped down whatever social structures got in my way. I always imagined my assaults on demonic forces as the wonderful wielding of a sword of justice instead of as upset with disowned aspects of myself projected onto others. Pretentiously profound, abrasively I eradicated any gloss of social interaction that might seem shallow or artificial.

Shiva's ascetic yogic posture was best suited to his reclusive dwelling in the mountain wilderness. I also avoided the communal company of ordinary valley villagers. My own intuitive introverted eccentricity and detachment were best suited to times spent almost exclusively in solitude or in the strangely select company of others odd enough to earn my acceptance as intimate friends or immediate family. I was in the world but not of it. Every two or three years I made the correct mistake of accepting an invitation to a party in order to reconfirm my being a misfit bound not to belong in the world of ordinary people. Like Shiva, I defined myself as fierce, terrible, lord and master of my own dark inner space.

Entering into the social world of ordinary people, Shiva's appearance was off-putting in its uncivilized rudeness of matted hair and animal-skin garb. I settled for keeping my hair at a studiously casual, unfashionable length and willingly wearing a beard when it was not yet quite in fashion. These self-styled stigmata implicitly announced to others that I was not to be expected to behave myself. I never wanted to seem appropriately attired. No matter what the social occasion, I costumed myself in boots, blue jeans, and dark sweat shirts, adorned only by esoteric emblems, bold pendants such as an ankh carved out of a walrus tusk, or a ferocious dragon tooled in brass. Dark-colored wide leather wristbands; broad, boldly buckled belts; and a Tibetan bracelet crudely crafted in copper, brass, and nickel-silver were intended to announce to strangers my warlike willingness to battle anyone who would take me on.

During those years of seeing myself as a Shiva-like savior, I judged nothing I did or said as outrageous so long as it was offered in the service of my arrogantly inflated ego ideal of "unmanageable integrity." As a self-styled eccentric outlaw hero, I wished only to strike unexpectedly, to rectify wrongs, and to disappear into the sunset, leaving ordinary people to wonder, "Who was that masked man?"

In my earlier writings,[1] I have described in detail samples of my most shamelessly disruptive showing off. Till now it had not occurred to me to expose the one instance in which even I was distressed by my capacity for disruption. I was working as chief psychologist for a community mental health center. At a weekly staff meeting, the chief psychiatrist announced that the clinic had been invited to send a representative to appear on a local radio program. Knowing that the talk-show host had a reputation for provocatively disarming and embarrassing his guests, no one on the staff wanted to volunteer for the job. Imagining as I did that I could handle anything, I seized the opportunity to undertake another challenge.

At first I felt excited. Knowing that the host was likely to ask unexpected questions, there was no way for me to prepare even an outline of what I might wish to say. But as the time for the broadcast drew near, I found myself growing unaccountably and uncharacteristically tense. I began to have difficulty falling asleep at night. Gradually my apprehension evolved into full-blown panic.

I feared that I might get angry enough to blow up on the air and tell the host, "Fuck off!" Were I speaking only for myself, that would have felt all right to me. However, representing the clinic and the interests of the patients we served, I was afraid I would jeopardize the welfare of the people I imagined depended on me to save them.

My anticipatory anguish continued to spiral out of control until I came to recognize the secret wish hidden beneath the fear I felt. Relief came in a dream where, appearing onstage before thousands of people, I smiled to myself, turned my back to the audience, and dropped my pants. The next morning I understood the dream to mean that my fear of behaving with outrageous inappropriateness on the air was a self-denying cover for my desire to disrupt the whole world in one swell foop. As soon as that insight emerged, my anxiety abated. When the time came for the broadcast, I was calm and confident, managing the show-host's provocative questions with ease and detachment. With my destructiveness consciously contained, I was able to carry out creatively the assignment I had undertaken.

Shiva is the god of the crossroads whose particular polarities are expressed in a taut tension between the opposites of destruction and creation, asceticism and involvement, and anger and compassion. My own seeming detachment was belied by my readiness to challenge anyone who took a stand or who seemed deliberately to avoid taking a stand. Without thinking about anything except my next petty moral victory, I shot from the hip. Though intending to help others, too often I hurt them. Posing as a healer both of social injustice and psychological dishonesty, I deceived myself by passionately projecting onto them my own internal failings. Becoming a helpful healer required gradually recognizing myself as one of the walking wounded as fully flawed as those I targeted. It took a long, long time.

Prior to that transformation, my Shiva-savior stance seemed to require my disrupting others doing as they pleased. Imagining that I was sacrificing myself for their own good, often I inflated my own ego by demonstrating that I could destroy what I saw as their complacency. Shameless and shocking, self-indulgent and sardonic, I interrupted other people by moralistic meddling in what I saw as their mischief.

My favorite Shiva creation myth[2,3] is that of his interruptive intervention as an archer. He came upon Brahma in his incarnation as Prajapati, the Lord of Generation who as Father Heaven was fired with desire for his own daughter, Dawn. In attempting to escape her father's incestuous passion, Dawn transformed herself into a doe and ran off. In response, her father became a buck and pursued her.

As he was about to take his perverse pleasure with her, Prajapati became aware of an archer aiming his arrow at him. Frightened, the father asked to be let alone, offering Shiva the bribe of appointing him Lord of Animals. Intent on interrupting consummation of this incestuous passion, Shiva shot an arrow at the father. Because he was internally divided by the opposites within himself, Shiva delayed a moment too long, and the arrow struck the father too late to prevent his seed from falling. Shifting from his destructive to his creative aspect, Shiva caught the seed in his mouth and sowed it upon the earth. Surrounding the seed, he provided the protection needed to allow the generation of humankind.

Shiva's intended interruption of the consummation of the father's passion can be seen as an attempt to disrupt the resolution of a period in which all things are simultaneous and uncreated into a segment of the circle during which unbroken time begins again. He knew that the resumption of sequential easy time would reintroduce the temptation to attachment to consequences. Shiva's commitment to the timeless chaos of the circle's break is an expression of his efforts to free his followers from the contingencies of life. When once again his people face hard times, he attempts to eliminate the harsh necessities that inevitably interrupt episodes of easy living that each of us enjoys as if they could be unending.

At these times Shiva appears to save those who suffer needlessly. As an ascetic yogi, he arrives to announce that it is only our attachment to wanting things our own way that makes us unhappy. He himself has practiced the austerities that allow experiencing each moment as it comes without hoping to hold on to the inevitable passage of ephemeral pleasures. Shiva teaches the detachment that would free his followers from the grief of disappointment over changes they cannot control. The release from suffering that he models for his devotees is the discipline of Yoga, the yoke that frees.

My own teaching of psychotherapy was for many years founded on Shiva's detached attitude of seemingly simple austerity. Again and again, young therapists came to me for supervision, complaining:

> I'm stuck. For a while the work was going well, but now we're at an impasse. My patient has reached a plateau. He (or she) is blocking and I can't seem to get him over his resistance. I've tried and tried to figure out why he's doing that but he's fighting me all the way.

It's difficult for the therapist to understand that "a therapeutic impasse" is simply a time when the therapist is trying to make a patient do something that the patient is not ready to do. By focusing on the patient's "progress," the therapist engages in a needless power struggle. Getting hung up on how well or how poorly the therapist is doing also distractedly drains his or her own creative energy from the work. The most ready resolution for these deadly problems is the therapist's shifting focus to the basic therapeutic techniques. Getting out of that awful, stuck place requires that the therapist turn attention away from the patient's behavior, away from concern with self-image, and toward concentration simply on doing impeccable work.

Shiva's discipline of Yoga is one way of getting unstuck. Though I no longer practice meditation regularly, as a metaphor it serves me well in getting beyond being stuck trying to get my own way in my work as a psychotherapist (as well as in the rest of life).

I remember my own early instruction in the Yoga of breath-counting. To prepare myself, each day I was to sit comfortably for short periods at regular times. My mind would be cleared by focusing all of my attention on the edges of my nostrils, at that place where the breath is exhaled.

My teacher told me: "You need only breathe in and out quietly and regularly, concentrating on that point. Each time you exhale, you count to yourself, 'one . . . , two . . . , three . . . ,' and so on. When you get to 'ten,' begin again."

It sounded easy enough. But my teacher went on to warn me of the demons with which I would struggle: "You'll find that you begin 'one . . . , two . . . ,' and then the thoughts will come. And so it will be 'one . . . , two . . . ,' and suddenly you'll think, 'This isn't working!' At that point you must go back to one. You try it again: 'one . . . , two . . . ,' and all at once, 'Now I'm getting it.' Back to one. Still other thoughts will arise to distract you. Discomforts and temptations will emerge as distractions ('My legs are getting stiff,' or 'My ass itches') and temptations ('I wonder what it would be like to go to bed with that woman I met yesterday,' or 'Someday I'll be truly enlightened'). Each time you need only go back to one."

At first I did not see why I would have to go back to one. All I needed to do would be to overcome those thoughts. As if reading my mind, my teacher went on: "You'll be tempted to try to dismiss the thoughts, simply to get rid of them. That won't work. It's just another trap. All that will happen is that you'll get deeper and deeper into your insistence that you can overcome the struggles. The only solution each time is to go back to one."

It began not to sound so easy. I started out with the notion that I was certain to go through the series up to ten and begin again. I could do series after series. Should I count them? "Not to worry," said my teacher. "During the first year of breathing meditation, most people do not get beyond four or five. And then come the thoughts, and again it's always back to one."

It is the same in the practice of psychotherapy. Again and again the therapist is trapped in willful attachment to how he or she is doing, to how the patient is progressing, to the results, to getting his or her own way. All arise as distractions from the work. In each case the solution is to go back to one. But first the therapist must have prepared a setting in which the basic work can be done. What's more, he or she must have a clear idea of what is to be done and how to do it, or else there is no "one" to which to go back.

Years ago, I wrote a detailed description of how I do therapy.[4] I offered it only as a guide—not as the ways to work, but simply as my ways of working. I cautioned the reader: "My ways need not be yours, though some may suit your own path." I offered them to encourage means of becoming ever clearer about the fundamentals of an individual's special style of work.

To free oneself from the bondage of attachment to its results, it is necessary to be clear about the work. When we do not concentrate one-pointedly on the basic work, we pay attention instead to the patient's "progress," or to our own egobound evaluations ("Look how well [or how badly] I'm doing."). Neither path benefits either the patient or the therapist. At the point of impasse, the only thing that helps is to go back to one.

But to find the way back, the therapist first must know what "one" is for him or her in particular. Clarity about what one does, about how the therapy is run is absolutely necessary. It is sometimes useful, creative, and fun to vary from the basic parameters of the work. But first the therapist must know the personal base line from which to vary. Otherwise, how is it possible to know when to return home and how to find the way back?

Learning to go back to one by returning to fundamentals of the work, the therapist is helped to feel comfortable by simply being in charge of the therapy and leaving the patient in charge of his or her own life. Out of this comes the best work—that alliance in the absence of blame in which healing can occur. Only then can the therapist offer the expert services of a professional guide and so avoid the impasse born of the presumption of thinking that the therapist knows what is best for the patient. By concentrating on the therapeutic work the therapist gets unstuck, leaving the patient free to discover what he or she wants out of life, how to go about getting it, and at what cost. It is the patient who must choose just how he or she is to live. When the therapist helps the patient to be happier without needing the patient to change, the therapist's own impeccable work is reward enough.

It is the same with Yoga. At first each seeker practices as a path toward the goal of spiritual liberation. Initially taken on by the beginner as a means to an end, the burdensome efforts of self-discipline are later pursued for their own intrinsic rewards by the more advanced yogi.

Many Westerners think of Yoga as nothing more than a peculiar system of breathing exercises accompanied by grotesque physical postures. Classical Yoga practices are something more than holding your breath and standing on your head. They have little to do with its Americanized popularization as a gymnastic cult of physical beauty and prolonged youth.

Some Westerners imagine that the practice of Yoga is an Oriental form of magic, a vehicle for attaining occult powers. It is not that special powers do not accrue for the yogi; rather it is simply that these *siddhis* are not what they appear to be. The notorious Indian rope trick is a good example of the cheap magic practiced by fakirs who use Yoga powers for exploitative purposes.

Some years ago an account appeared in the *Chicago Tribune*[5] that told of two Americans who witnessed such a performance while traveling together in northern India. They both watched as the rope appeared to unwind itself toward the sky. Just as the conjurer's assistant began to climb the rope, one of the Americans, an artist, made a rapid sketch of the scene. His companion, who was carrying a camera, photographed what he saw. Later the photographs showed only a crowd gathered around the fakir, with the boy beside him, and the rope at their feet. Nothing had been suspended but the judgment of the audience. Suggestion or induced hallucination? Perhaps. Levitation? Not according to the photographic evidence!

Among the other siddhis or "marvelous powers" that develop in the practice of Yoga are those phenomena we in the West categorize as parapsychological: extrasensory perception, telepathy, psychokinesis, and perhaps even outside-the-body experiences. They parallel the altered states of consciousness and dramatic instant emotional catharses induced in patients by some Western psychotherapists.

The Indian writers who believe that siddhis exist view them as distractions from the right practice of concentration and meditation. These by-products serve only as obstacles to enlightenment and as stumbling blocks in the path to liberation.

An anecdote began circulating in Berkeley, California, about Carlos Castaneda's recent visit to Yogi Chen, an elderly Chinese practitioner of esoteric Buddhism and something of a local saint. Castaneda, it seems, told Yogi Chen that he was now being taught how to produce a "double" of himself. Was there anything similar in Chen's traditions? Of course, said Yogi Chen, there were methods for producing up to six emanations of oneself, "But why bother? Then you only have six times as much trouble."[6] Equivalent psychotherapeutic "magic" creates similar distractions in the treatment process.

How are we to understand a path of self-development that considers the acquisition of the power to perform miracles as no more than a trivial distraction from spiritual discipline? This is not true of Yoga alone. None of the Indian philosophies and mystic techniques has either power or "truth" as its goal. The West may pursue progress through knowledge and power. The East seeks only deliverance from struggle.

Yoga of one sort or another may be found in all

Eastern spiritual paths. In each case the goals are the same: the raising of consciousness beyond the distinction between the watcher and the watched; awareness free from desire. The goal is no less than total deliverance from needless struggle by means of nonattachment; it is knowing that concern with making things happen is meaningless.

The acquisition of knowledge and power in the absence of the benign detachment that comes with spiritual maturity is a hazardous stage in any path of self-development. The hazards are most vivid in those paths that involve the mastery of violence. Here are some instructive words from the pen of a black belt adept in the Japanese martial art of karate:

> I think that the most dangerous time for most Karateka [students of karate] is when they have reached the brown belt level. At this grade, they are strong and fast, and notoriously rough in free fighting. They are accurate with their blows, and deliver them with power, certainly enough to maim or kill. They have learned to focus, and they have begun to learn fighting spirit. All of this they have learned, but they have not learned calmness and tolerance and the state of empty-mind that is brought about by further intensive practice.[7]

The cautions offered by this master of "the gentle art" of karate hold for the practices of Yoga and psychotherapy as well. Once young therapists gain an understanding of personality dynamics and a repertoire of disarming therapeutic ploys, they enter a dangerous phase. Their focused need to change the patient takes precedence over an unattached readiness to offer the excellent and expert techniques that provide an accepting atmosphere within which the patient might grow at his or her own pace. It is a time of struggle between therapist and patient, of therapeutic impasses, and of needless suffering for both.

Understanding the discrediting of such powers in the context of Yoga begins with the Indian conception of life as a "wheel of sorrows" turning from birth through the suffering of this life to death and rebirth into yet another round of pain. As Buddha proclaimed: "All is anguish, all is ephemeral."

The misery of human life is due to the ignorance that attributes substance to the illusion that is this life and to the attachment that leads us to try to hold on to the impermanent things of this life. To whatever extent we focus our longing on getting our own way, on doing to achieve results, on holding on to things beyond our control—to that extent we are trapped in needless suffering.

Paradoxically, the Indian conception of universal suffering does not lead to a pessimistic philosophy founded on despair. Suffering is not a tragedy. It is a cosmic necessity. Yet each person has a chance to become free of it. For each individual, karma is the crucial pivot.

Karma is the conception that each act has consequences. Our circumstances in this life are the consequences of actions in our earlier lives. How we live in this life will determine what our next life will hold in store. It is not necessary to believe in reincarnation to apply this view to our own lives. Even if we have only one life, we create our karma as we live it.

We can gradually liberate ourselves from needless suffering. It is possible to affect our future karma by doing the work on our selves, by raising our consciousness beyond the ignorance of attachment to the results of our efforts. I only get to keep that which I am prepared to give up. In Western terms, virtue is its own reward. There is no hope of redemption in doing good in order to be saved. Only by doing good for its own sake, without seeking reward, can I attain salvation.

For the patient, psychotherapy may be seen as an attempt to improve karma in this life. The therapist helps the patient to heighten awareness of the consequences of actions and of the price of willful attachment to getting one's own way. In part the therapist offers this in the role of the guru. He or she shows the patient ways to unhook from old patterns by the liberation of self from attachment to the neurotic past.

The therapist not only offers treatment techniques, but the model of nonattachment to the results of his or her own therapeutic efforts as well. Both the practices and the nonattachment are crucial to the process. Baba Ram Dass describes the Karma Yoga of such offerings by saying:

> . . . the only thing you have to offer another human being, ever, is your own state of being . . . everything, whether you're cooking food or doing therapy or being a student or being a lover, you are only doing, you're only manifesting how evolved a consciousness you are. That's what you're doing with another human being. That's the only dance there is! . . . Consciousness . . . means freedom from attachment. . . . You realize that the only thing you have to do for another human being is to keep yourself really straight, and then do whatever it is you do.[8]

How can Yoga help us to find deliverance? Indian philosophy provides two avenues. The earlier pathway

of self-development is called Samkhya, which means
"discrimination" or liberation through knowledge. Samkhya provides a basic theoretical exposition of human
nature. If a person is devoted in good faith to acquiring
his metaphysical knowledge, he or she may become
liberated.

But Samkhya serves as a pathway to release from
spiritual bondage only to a few rare individuals. For
most of us it serves as a preliminary preparation for the
real work of the practice of Yoga itself. Classical Yoga
begins where Samkhya ends, standing as practice to
theory, as act to thought, as reality to fantasy.

The term "Yoga" derives etymologically from a root
meaning "to bring under the yoke." Yoga offers the
seeker the opportunity to unify his or her spirit with the
universal soul, to become one with the way of life by
experiencing an arranged curriculum of self-training in
ascetic and meditational practices. It is at the same time
both a discipline of austerities and a path of liberation.
Yoga is the yoke that frees as it bridges the broken circle
of experienced time.

There are two primary divisions of these practices—
Raja Yoga, the royal path of cultivating the mind and
the personality; and Hatha Yoga, the mastery of breathing and other physiological functions that aims at liberation through purification and development of mastery
over the body.[9] In attempting to develop a metaphor for
the nonattached practice of psychotherapy, I have focused almost exclusively on Shiva's Raja Yoga, the Yoga
of the will, particularly on the practices of meditation,
and on Krishna's Karma Yoga, the way of action and
loving work.

Meditation begins with concentration. At first this
sounds simple enough. All you have to do is fix your

attention on a single point. It might be on the tip of the nose, on a thought or an action, on a holy saying, or on an image of God. This simple exercise turns out to be enlightening in its unexpected difficulty. Ram Dass[10] describes it as equivalent to trying to tame a wild jungle elephant by putting an iron band around its leg and chaining it to a post in the ground. When like your wandering mind, the elephant realizes that you are trying to tame it, it gets wilder than it ever was in the jungle. It pulls and it pulls and it can hurt its leg to the point of bleeding or breaking before it finally gives in and becomes tame. This roughly is the tradition of meditation.

It is not possible to pursue the meditational path of liberation without straying. Concentration in the practice of Yoga, psychotherapy, or any other spiritual folk art is a matter of developing the ability to do one thing at a time. In the practice of meditation, straying from this goal has popularly been characterized as "itching, twitching, and bitching." Because most psychotherapy lacks the physical demands of Yoga and because psychotherapy is interpersonal, the distractions with which therapists must struggle are more focused on needless evaluative comparisons between how the therapist is doing and how he or she should be doing, or on the reciprocal point of how the patient is progressing and how the therapist thinks the patient should be progressing.

Nonetheless, the problems are fundamentally the same. It is easy for the practitioner of Yoga or psychotherapy to think of other things, to become distracted with remembrances of times past and of other places. Or concentration may be lost by straying into future concerns about how all this is going to turn out. Again, the required correction is back to one.

Even seemingly present-oriented self-consciousness

serves as a distraction if there is any element of comparison embedded within it. Comparisons are always deadly, whether they pivot around how I am different from or the same as another, or merely around how I am different now from how I was, or how I will be at another time.

The goal is to have your whole being concentrated in what you are doing at the moment. Saint Anthony said it well: "The prayer of the monk is not perfect until he no longer realizes himself or the fact that he is praying.[11]

The therapist, too, does the best work when not trying to change the patient, or even trying to experience doing psychotherapy. The therapist becomes the work. The therapist is the psychotherapy, and it all just seems to flow. The irony is that when the work goes this well, it is difficult to recapture in retrospect just what it was you did right.

A parable of Sri Ramakrishna demonstrates that first we must learn to concentrate; only then may we gain a sense of what it feels like to be doing impeccable work:

> A disciple once came to a teacher to learn to meditate on God. The teacher gave him instructions, but the disciple soon returned and said that he could not carry them out; every time he tried to meditate, he found himself thinking about his pet buffalo. "Well then," said the teacher, "you meditate on that buffalo you're so fond of." The disciple shut himself up in a room and began to concentrate on the buffalo. After some days, the teacher knocked at his door and the disciple answered: "Sir, I am sorry I can't come out to greet you. This door is too small. My horns will be in the way." Then the teacher smiled and said: "Splen-

did! You have become identified with the object
of your concentration. Now fix that concentration
upon God and you will easily succeed."[12]

For most of us, one lifetime does not seem long
enough to attain a state of perfect concentration. As in
my work as a psychotherapist, in my personal life, too,
I get distracted, make mistakes, as again and again I lose
my way. I must learn to give myself permission to
blunder, to fail, and to make a fool of myself every day
for the rest of my life. I will do so in any case. Scolding
and self-recrimination are no more than further errors.
Instead, I can turn to the unconditional self-acceptance
of one of India's greatest discoveries: consciousness as a
witness. To do this I must surrender to the instructions
to:

> treat yourself as if you were a much-loved child
> that an adult was trying to keep walking on a
> narrow sidewalk. The child is full of energy and
> keeps running off to the fields on each side to pick
> flowers, feel the grass, climb a tree. Each time
> you are aware of the child leaving the path, you
> say in effect, "Oh, that's how children are. Okay,
> honey, back to the sidewalk," and bring yourself
> gently but firmly and alertly back to just looking. . . .
> "Oh, that's where I am now, back to work."[13]

LeShan's "back to work" is my "back to one." His
"just looking" is a reminder that if I am to tame the wild
elephant of my mind, I must not beat it. At first it was
not easy to get used to staying in one spot. Wildly
resisting by struggling to be somewhere else was painful
and self-destructive.

But willfully trying to force the elephant or my mind or my patient to stay calmly in a place in which either of these is not yet ready to stay is an exercise in futility and needless suffering. Instead I had to learn to witness the discomforting interruption and the tendency to stray, without longing, without coercion, and without blame.

> . . . when it comes up—it's like somebody who drops by for tea when you are trying to work on a manuscript. You say, "Hello, it's great to have you. Why don't you go into the kitchen and have tea with my wife (if she's not busy, too), and I'll be along later. I'm working on this manuscript." And then you go back to the manuscript.[14]

Honoring Shiva demands detachment at times of disruption. Whether it's the manuscript or the meditation or the work of psychotherapy, at such times I simply need to go back to one.

NOTES

1. Sheldon Kopp, *The Pickpocket and the Saint: Free Play of Imagination*, "Shameless Compensations" (New York: Bantam Books, 1983), pp. 139–58.

2. Stella Kramrisch, *The Presence of Siva* (Princeton, N.J.: Princeton University Press, 1981).

3. Wendy Doniger O'Flaherty, *Siva: The Erotic Ascetic* (London: Oxford University Press, 1981); first published in London and New York for the

School of Oriental and African Studies, 1973, under the title *Asceticism and Eroticism in the Mythology of Siva*.

4. Sheldon Kopp, *Back to One: A Practical Guide for Psychotherapists* (Palo Alto, Calif.: Science and Behavior Books, 1977). This description of Shiva-like self-supervision was included in a somewhat different form, pp. 13–22.

5. Ernest Wood, *Seven Schools of Yoga: An Introduction* (Wheaton, Ill.: The Theosophical Publishing House, 1973), pp. 1–2.

6. Daniel Noel, ed., *Seeing Castaneda: Reactions to the "Don Juan" Writings of Carlos Castaneda* (New York: G.P. Putnam's Sons, 1976), p. 59.

7. C.W. Nicol, *Moving Zen: Karate as a Way to Gentleness* (New York: William Morrow & Company, 1975), p. 93.

8. Baba Ram Dass, *The Only Dance There Is* (Garden City, N.Y.: Anchor Press/Doubleday & Company, 1974), p. 6.

9. Wood, op. cit. See this work for a discussion of the full range of schools of Yoga.

10. Baba Ram Dass, op. cit., p. 118.

11. Lawrence LeShan, *How to Meditate: A Guide to Self-Discovery* (New York: Bantam Books, 1974), p. 59.

12. Patanjali, *How to Know God: The Yoga Aphorisms of Patanjali*, translated with a new commentary by Swami Prabhavananda and Christopher Isherwood (New York: New American Library, 1953), p. 126.

13. LeShan, p. 54.

14. Baba Ram Dass, op. cit., p. 120.

Chapter 5

Kali at the Crossroads

Shiva is a god of contradictions who maintains the tension between the wildness in people and nature on the one hand, and the world of art and cosmic order on the other. In his hands, he carries not only fiery arrows and a bow but healing remedies as well. Fierce intermediary of the inevitable disruptions in all our lives, he teaches us how to heal the very wounds he inflicts.

Paradoxical in all his pursuits, Shiva is known as an "erotic ascetic"[1] whose eternally erect penis manifests metaphorically the power of his detachment. This symbol of unspent passion represents the taming of otherwise unbounded emotion.

Like the other gods of the Hindu pantheon, he is both patriarchal and androgynous. Each male god has a feminine aspect. It is she who activates the energy that allows the passive patriarch his power. The feminine aspects of the gods ordinarily appear as mere appendages of their divine spouses. Most seem to have neither personalities nor stories of their own. Shiva's wife is an exception. Though she is often simply seen as the goddess Devi, like Shiva, she, too, is a collection of contrary beneficent and ferocious personalities.

As Parvati she compels his power to its compassionate calling. This daughter of the Himalayas awakens Shiva from immersion in ascetic austerities so he can respond to people in times of need.

Impatiently passionate, it was difficult for Parvati to constrain her adoration while waiting beside a husband perpetually immersed in asceticism. Shiva sat so deeply lost in meditation that he was unaware of her presence. Seductively, Parvati covered his eyes. To counter her playfulness, a third eye emerged in Shiva's forehead, allowing him transcendent vision that could dispel dogmas and resist temptations.

To aid Parvati in seducing Shiva away from his consuming contemplations, the other gods had sent personifications of love and pleasure. When Parvati approached her husband, Love drew his bow. At the very moment when the arrow was aimed, she was seductively awakening Shiva. With a burning flash of his third eye, he consumed Love. Pleasure and Parvati despaired that both her husband and Love would be forever lost.

In her time of desolation, a divine voice promised Parvati that some day Love's body would unite with her husband's soul. Weary of waiting for an end to Shiva's indifference, his weary wife undertook the life of a hermit. Living alone in the forest, for years she practiced her own austerities.

One day a young Brahman visited to celebrate her faithful devotion. He tried to persuade her to return to the world of people. She became angry at his tempting her to be unfaithful. Then the young man revealed that he himself was Shiva, returning to offer her his love. Parvati persisted in her detachment until he promised to reclaim the body of erotic Pleasure in a permanently tense merger with his transcendent yogic soul. Not until he agreed did Parvati yield to Shiva's desire. Their long-awaited embrace made the whole world tremble.

In most of the Hindu myths[2] divine feminine aspects appear as energizing consorts of the gods. Though lovingly devoted, their existence is always auxiliary. Unlike Parvati, they are not sufficiently evolved to be married to a god.

Even more atypically, the feminine aspect of Shiva is the one goddess who is at times totally independent of the god. As the Great Mother she often acts on her own without the authority of husband, consort, or lover. She can be arbitrarily fierce and warlike. In her darkest forms, as the inaccessible Durga or the black one, Mother Kali,[3] the disruptive goddess Devi is devouringly ferocious. Bloodthirsty and cruelly insatiable, she crushes and devours her enemies.

In one legend, Kali first appears as Sleep, then as the dream of Night, and ultimately as Death itself. Even in this softer side, she acts as the indifferently devouring mother of sorrows whose indiscriminate onslaught inevitably exhausts and ages us all. Acting impersonally, she edges us toward the dying that is the ultimate end of every life. Utterly undiscriminating as the feminine form of Time, she gradually wears us down with the impersonal necessities to be met in everyday living. Challenging the individual arrogance of our inflated egos, she reveals the world in all its harsh, indifferent, and seemingly capricious aspects.

In her more passionate moments she can appear as horribly catastrophic. In one Hindu myth, her fierce emergence takes the form of the bloodthirsty mother born of anger. This ferocious aspect occurred when the demon Mahisa appeared in the form of a buffalo seeming so omnipotent that he oppressed the gods and vanquished them in battle. Then the dark shadow side of the goddess Devi emerged to combat and defeat the demonic buffalo. Once released, the passionate goddess was unstoppable. She deferred neither to god nor man, operating entirely on her own. Needing neither husband nor consort, she bowed to no one.

In the midst of battle with the buffalo, the goddess became openly enraged. Out of Devi's wrath-filled brow came Kali. Utterly uncontrollable, she was fury run riot. Her insatiable hunger devoured everything it encountered. In this ferocious aspect, the goddess became a devastating predator, shattering and consuming all that opposed her.

When the sweet and benign spouse of Shiva emerges as the ferociously independent and unmanageable Kali, the great goddess delights in destruction. In her kindness, the goddess serves figuratively as good fortune personally bestowing wealth and plenty during periods of prosperity. Intermittently, in her primordial wildness, as Kali she may manifest herself as misfortune dealing out the disasters that can threaten anyone with annihilation at any time.

Like life itself, whether fierce or friendly, she is entirely unpredictable. It is as impossible to prepare for Kali's coming as it is to control her once she arrives. Shiva can be expected to annihilate the universe whenever a cycle calls for the inevitable epic of the destruction of evil. Kali's arbitrary disruptions erupt unexpectedly at any time. She is the raw power of life whose untamed energy operates without discipline or direction, unpredictably disrupting episodes of easy living with the awful horror of troubled times. We take our good fortune as it comes, complacently expecting it to continue without interruption. Suddenly Kali appears, mounted on the lion of nature's bestial ferocity. Unexpectedly we find ourselves having sickened, aged, or been battered by an unexpected episode of disappointment or death. Once again Kali makes us aware of how helplessly we encounter life's unmanageable onslaughts.

There is no order to these arbitrary interruptions of easy living. We are not necessarily being rightly punished for wrongdoing. Nor need these disruptions reflect some reasonable righting of our errors in judgment. Instead we must contend with uncalled-for calamities in the form of random ravages of life addressed: "to whom it may concern." Life laughs at our complacency, our sense of having it all together, and our illusions of omnipotence and invulnerability.

At those terrible moments, the sound we hear is the horrible howling laugh of Kali as she envelops us in her inescapably malevolent maw. She is awful to behold. Her appallingly emaciated flesh speaks of insatiable hunger. Fangs protrude and a tongue lolls out of her wide and gaping bloodthirsty mouth. There is no escape from the targeting gaze of her deep-sunk, blood-red eyes. Standing ugly and naked before us, her shriveled flesh is adorned only with a necklace of human skulls and a girdle of severed hands. Carrying a sword, a noose, and a skull-topped club, she beats down and chews up anyone she comes upon, grinding them out of existence with her teeth, swallowing or spitting them out as she chooses.

Neither reason nor right and wrong can rein her ravages. This untamed, uncaring, uncompromising force is Time itself. Kali can be understood as the symbol of hard times that cannot be avoided. No one escapes the harsh realities of sickness, old age, and death, or the arbitrary disruptions of inevitable change, disillusionment, and disappointment.

Surrounded by jackals and other unholy scavengers, like a rapacious wolf, Kali hunts us down in those aspects of life that cannot be kept at bay nor successfully circumvented. Relentless and without pity, her fickle, indifferent unpredictability cannot be mastered but must never be ignored. The only comfort she offers lies is our awareness and acceptance that at any moment one of life's awful annihilating blows may fall.

Watching and waiting for her coming, we may waste our lives by worrying away those times when living is easy. But we are equally endangered if we ignore the ravenous rages to which she may subject us at any moment. Pretending that we are safe from the unpredictably destructive disruptions that can come at any time leaves us even less ready to recover from their ravages when unpredictably but inevitably Kali comes upon us once again. The harshness of life's hard times cannot be avoided, but aware and accepting of their inescapable harshness, we are better suited to survive until the broken circle of time takes another turn into the next era of easy living.

As an intuitive introvert, my own resources for adapting to disruptive changes are irrational and internal. Enduring Kali's onslaughts is a matter of allowing my dreams to inform me. Soon after I became ill some years ago, I dreamed that I was on Cape Ann, the northern headland of Massachusetts Bay. My own cape, where I most often spend my summers, is the southern head, Cape Cod, and the lovely islands that surround it. That southern cape of easy living is warm and rich and green and soft, but not so Cape Ann. The northern cape of hard times is very different. I've spent time on the northern cape, and there are qualities about it that draw me back, but for the most part it has been a place I have avoided. Cape Ann is a rugged, craggy seascape; angular, covered with scant, scrubby foliage; dark, wind-blown, dangerous-looking territory. In its own way it is a strikingly beautiful seascape, but awfully ominous.

The dream began with my having emerged from a small, rugged beach cottage such as one might find on Cape Ann. I stepped through the doorway of the cottage and out into the night. I don't know where I was headed, but I began to walk slowly across a great open barren wilderness, a vast tundra, not unlike the cremation grounds in which Kali is most comfortable. I followed the ambling footpaths; there were no roads. I wandered for a while until I had come quite a distance from the cottage.

Suddenly the night became very, very dark. I don't know now whether I realized this in the dream or whether it came as an explanation I offered myself after I had awakened, but it seemed to me that the moon had suddenly passed behind dark clouds. As I stood there in the sullen darkness, unable to see which way to go, a piece of my everyday anxiety suddenly flooded the dream.

One of the residuals of my brain surgery is that my balance is very uncertain. Taken by the inertia of my own movement, I'm inclined to topple over. My body compensates for this during the day, and although I suffer from fatigue as a consequence, I can make my way. But at night, when it's dark, my kinesthetic feedback is limited, distorted, betraying. Without daytime's visual cues, I need to carry a light or to hold someone's hand. Holding someone's hand was a difficult surrender for me. For a while I stubbornly resisted that. I no longer do so.

In the dream, finding myself in the darkness, suddenly I felt like a fool. I said to myself, "What the hell are you doing out here without a flashlight? How stupid to leave the house without the light you needed." For a moment I stood there and debased myself for having made a mistake. Then I decided I must go back to the house, I must get a light, or I simply wouldn't be able to manage. I was afraid I would stumble, fall, and hurt myself, or worse yet, that I would be lost forever on that vast, dark plain. I tried to find my way back to the house. I couldn't see at all. I moved my feet, shuffling them about, trying to find the footpath. I found that just feeling about with my feet, I couldn't really tell where the path was. Like an animal, I got down on all fours. Patting around with my hands, I tried to discover where the path lay so that I could find my way back to the house.

While I was scrounging around down there, I became aware of another presence. I was not alone. At first I thought it must be a dog. I respond counterphobically to my fear of dogs, an anxiety I don't understand and of which I am only inferentially aware. I don't know it directly. Dogs don't *seem* to frighten me, but I know that I am a bit rougher with them than I need to be. Rather than make friends, I try to intimidate them. In the dream I reassured myself that if this was a dog, it was only a dog, and I wasn't too upset about that.

Still, I remained on the alert. As I watched, the beast drew closer. Soon I could see the intense gleam of glaring, yellow eyes. All at once I knew it was not a dog. The beast I faced was a wolf.

Characteristically, I reacted as in my waking life. The first thing that occurred to me was, "Oh, I see, now my task is to kill this wolf." But then uncharacteristic things began to happen in the dream. I suddenly had a new look at myself and I thought, "That's absurd. It's too crazy! How can I kill a wolf with my bare hands, on its own turf, in the darkness, at a time when I can't even walk safely?"

And then came a second, still more startling wave of revelation. Suddenly I had a new understanding of what

I must do. I knew then that *I must make friends with this wolf.*[4]

Continued immersion in the dreamwork reclamation of projections can itself result in the emergence of yet another hidden aspect of personality and experience. After a time, we may become aware of the inner guide who is the dreaming self. As Jung tells us:

> Within each one of us there is another whom we do not know. He speaks to us in dreams and tells us how differently *he* sees us from how *we* see ourselves. When we find ourselves in an insolubly difficult situation, this stranger in us can sometimes show us a light which is more suited than anything else to change our attitude fundamentally, namely just that attitude which had led us into the difficult situation.[5]

The focus of my own shifting attention alternates between dedicated devotion to my true self and deceitful collaboration with my false self. During the periods of self-betrayal, I deliberately ignore all coded communications from my own dreaming self. Fearful that they will expose my fraudulence, I refuse to listen to the helpful nightly messages from this secret ally. Whenever I am willing and able to listen to my dreaming self, my daytime life becomes clearer and richer. Sometimes it even becomes easier. Undistorted by reason, logic, and conventional wisdom, my night vision affords a clear perspective as far as the imagination can see.

At first I did not recognize that inner guide as it appeared within my dream encounter with the wolf.[6] My most immediate level of understanding of that dream was as the revelation of projections of some significant aspects of my shadow side. At that interpretive level, the darkness of the night mirrored how vast and ominous I imagined the dark side of myself that is hidden from my awaking awareness. The Cape Ann seascape is the hard, cold, cruelly gothic aspects of my personality.

Usually I pictured myself as a decent, generous human being. At the time of the dream, I could understand the wolf only as a projection of the evil hidden within me. What a shameless fraud I had been to pretend I was so good when, all the while, the real me was a rapacious beast. Reclaiming the wolf as my own dark brother shattered the surface complacency of my self-serving pretense of civilized virtue. Acknowledging my own predatory ways meant paying attention to aspects of my behavior that usually either I ignored or tried to justify. These deceptions allowed me to maintain an idealized image of myself as a heroic figure. As long as my pretense went unchallenged, I could deny my capacity for occasional brutality and/or my more frequent self-serving disregard for anyone's needs but my own.

This unbalanced interpretation of my dream made me feel awful. The destructively predatory nature of my wolf side threatened to discredit all I consciously valued about myself. I tried to redeem my battered self-esteem by forcing a more acceptable interpretation. My most consistently positive self-image was that of myself as psychotherapist who is a sort of Santa Claus to the bad children.

I could see that my dream held the promise of support for that more comfortable vision of myself. Hoping to renew my shaky self-esteem, I focused on a more promising underside of the archetypal wolf. Even my dark shadow had a bright shadow of its own. Though the wolf's primary image is that of a ravaging killer, the destroyer's double appears in the form of the wolf as nurturing mother. The complementary image of myself

as having been a feral child allowed me to identify
lovingly with the bright shadow side of the wolf as
mother of outcasts.

This maternal aspect of the dream projection was
more congruent with my idealized image of myself. The
legendary wolf nursed Romulus and Remus so that they
might eventually found Rome. As a therapist I have
often imagined myself as the good mother who rescues
banished children and restores their rightful heritage.

Temporarily reassured, I set aside my growing preoc-
cupation with this wolf imagery and refocused my explorations on the continuing subtle dreams that subsequent nights provided. Many weeks passed before I
began to appreciate how much more my wolf dream
had to tell me. Without understanding why, again and
again I was drawn back to this encounter with my
shadow. I became obsessed with trying to decide once
and for all if this wolf dream was good news or bad
news. Was I to understand it as an indictment of my
evil nature or as a confirmation of my decency? It was
not until I surrendered to the realization that my questions were unanswerable that I began to understand that
the shift in contradictory interpretations was itself a
commentary on who I am. Just as the shifts in cycles of
the broken circle of my life alternate allegiances among
the many gods that manage my course, the wolf of my
dreams was mercurial and many-sided. Once unmasked
at the crossroads, the changing expressions of its Janus
face will not remain fixed.

When within the dream I first encountered the shape-
shifting creature, I mistook the wolf for a dog. The
following morning, I interpreted my "error" as a warn-
ing that the domestication of my own dangerous instinctual nature was tentative and unreliable. Lost and alone
in the vast darkness of the barren Cape Ann tundra, I

struggled with my need to make friends with this fearful beast. I felt myself forced to continue living the isolated life of the solitary lone wolf lest I risk losing my individual identity by choosing to run with the pack.[7]

Now I must come to understand and accept Kali's disruptively alternating aspects of both myself and my life. At times, like life itself, I am destructive and at other times nurturant, wild and tamed, solitary and communal. These unyieldingly contradictory aspects of my personality are as unresolvable as the hard times and the easy living that make up the broken circle of my life.

NOTES

1. Wendy Doniger O'Flaherty, *Siva: The Erotic Ascetic* (London and New York: Oxford University Press, 1973).

2. *Hindu Myths: A Source Book Translated from the Sanskrit*, Introduction by Wendy Doniger O'Flaherty (Baltimore: Penguin Books, 1975).

3. *Devi Mahatmyam (Glory of the Divine Mother): 700 Mantras on Sri Durga*, trans. Swami Jagadiswarananda (Mylapore, Madras: Sri Ramakrishna Math) (n.d.)

4. Sheldon Kopp, *Mirror, Mask and Shadow: The Risks and Rewards of Self-Acceptance* (New York: Bantam Books, 1982), pp. 24–26.

5. C. G. Jung, *Prakstische Seelenheilkunde Zentralplatt fur Psychotherapie* III: 184–187 (IX 1936) (review

of G. R. Heyer), in Yolande Jacobi, ed., *Psychological Reflections: An Anthology of the Writings of C.G. Jung* (New York: Harper & Row, 1961), p. 67.

6. Sheldon Kopp, *The Hanged Man: Psychotherapy and the Forces of Darkness* (Palo Alto, Calif.: Science and Behavior Books, 1974) (in a somewhat different version), pp. 25–27.

7. Ibid., pp. 175–77.

Chapter 6

Therapeutic Disruption

Shiva is the priest of the pariahs. Alienated by the ordinary community of those whose security arises out of the certainty of their social status, he surrounds himself with vampires, imps, and goblins. In his detachment, he is the ascetic Yoga instructor of others who have deliberately repudiated society. In his Kali aspect, he surrounds himself with fearful monsters and other impure outcasts.

As a therapist, much of my earlier work was guided by my commitment to the savage god Shiva and to his female counterpart, Kali. I considered my work to be a ministry to the misfits. Most often people who came to me for psychotherapy were outcasts who felt inadequate because they could not easily exist among the rest of the people of the community. The rest were self-styled eccentrics who lived in the world but were not of it.

I invited the entry of outcasts and eccentrics into the unsettling atmosphere of the office in which I practiced psychotherapy. Though I regretted the distress that these people suffered, I identified easily with the creative possibilities of the disruptive crises of their doubt, despair, and personal unrest. Paradoxically, it is exactly in these troubled times that people are sufficiently unsettled to allow opportunities for personal growth. If only they are able to accept the uneasy disturbance of their chronic complacency as a chance to change their prospects, unforeseen options arise. Instead of simply settling for an easing of pain, they may then explore opportunities for improving their lives offered by these disruptions.

Like everyone else (including the therapist), often the patient is inclined to act out of fear, rather than out of longing for growth. If not, psychological pilgrimages would always begin in an abundance of joy. More often they arise out of anguish and turmoil. People seek the guidance of a psychotherapist when distress and disruption in their lives result in their usual, self-limited, risk-avoiding ways of operating no longer paying off. Otherwise, we all are too ready to live with the familiar. Our usual ways need only keep things calm, no matter how colorless the rewards.

When patients enter therapy insisting that they want to change, more often than not what they really want is to remain the same while getting the therapist to make them feel better. The goal is to become a more effective neurotic so that the patient may have what he or she wants without the risk of experiencing anything unfamiliar. The security of known misery is preferred to the misery of newly met insecurity.

Given this all too human failing, the beginning patient may approach the therapist like a small child insisting on being taken care of by a good parent. It is as if the patient comes to the office saying, "My world is broken, and you have to fix it."

Because of this, as I began the Shiva work, my only goals were to take care of myself and to have fun. The patient had to provide the motive power of our interaction. It was as if I stood in the doorway of my office, waiting. The patient stumbled in, displaying a desperately dependent attempt to turn me into a caretaker. I stepped aside. Figuratively, the patient fell to the floor, disappointed and bewildered. That allowed a second chance to get up to try something new. If I was sufficiently skillful at this psychotherapeutic judo, and if the patient was sufficiently courageous and persistent, he or she might learn to become self-curious, to come to know me, and to begin to work out his or her own problems. The patient might then transform stubbornness into purposeful determination, exchanging this initial grab for safety into active pursuit of emotional adventure.

Wolf that I was, as mother of outcasts I made a place for every misfit who appeared for treatment. I never offered the maternal soothing that might enhance expectation of easy times. Instead I nurtured the independent toughness I imagined necessary to their dealing with the disruptions of the troubled times that life so often imposes. I encouraged them to experience obstacles as the raw materials out of which they might make stepping-stones. Much of what the patients experienced in themselves as corrupt, evil, brutal, and grotesque I redefined as having been incorrectly characterized only because of the contrast with their romantic notions of how wonderful they imagined a normal, natural person should be.

In a group therapy session one man told of being moved by a television program that depicted night predators as viewed through a naturalist's eye. Part of the story was about a pack of hyenas separating a hornless, month-old baby rhino from its mother so they could bring it down to be devoured. The baby rhino escaped.

The other group members were pleased and relieved at what seemed to me a Disney-like ending to the harrowing tale. But the teller went on to point out that though the baby had escaped for that night, at sunset on the following day the hyena pack would surely return for another try at the kill. Concerned murmurs from the other group members deplored the fate of the poor little rhino. I demanded to know why I was the only one rooting for the hyenas. Honoring Shiva, I insisted that the killers were also God's creatures.

Some of the patients tried to help me overcome my "defensive hard shell." Actually, I was only playing, in the savage way I sometimes did in my Shiva mode. Except when I was temporarily living out one or another aspect of my own Kali character, I felt no more committed to the predator than to the prey. In my ascetically distanced Shiva posture, the world seemed to me neither good nor bad. Life was just the way it was, a random, entropic nonpattern to which each of us brought our own meaning.

At that time, my emphasis in psychotherapy was almost entirely on effective interruption of old behaviors, precipitated by my therapeutic willingness to operate without engaging in romantic remedies. As in the rest of life, the encountering of other human beings in therapy continuously challenges the idealized images we all use to obscure our unspeakable thoughts and feelings. Each of us has been taught to maintain some measure of constraint of our primitive appetites, to present at least the appearance of sociability and self-control. However these virtues may vary from group to group, some signs of good character are supposed to be evident. Some element of respect for the other, of cooperation, of candor, and of modesty are expected. The masked dance of social accommodation demands at least a modicum of civilized demeanor.

We are expected to act as though we are not driven by powerful biological impulses nor haunted by dark, primitive images. Our surface social identities intentionally misrepresent our private selves. To maintain this successful sense of theater, social interaction is replete with ceremonies, conventions, and deferential dialogues that preserve the gloss of civilization. Whether intentional or inadvertent, infractions and deviations reveal underlying primitive instincts. Subject to censure, these must quickly be corrected by remedial interchanges. The powerfully primordial mythic images that influence human behavior remain hidden behind a façade of mannered reasonableness.

No matter how valuable, well-articulated, or strongly supported by philosophical and religious superstructures, our veneer of civilized characters remains thin and tentative. Post-Enlightenment people like to think of human nature as determined primarily by psychological and cultural forces. But hidden within each person is an imperial animal driven by dimensions determined by evolutionary development and mediated by genetic codes. Our uncivilized impulses activate instinctual patterns of mating, fighting, play, and politics. No matter how much we might prefer to view our interactions as noble expressions of higher sentiments, ideology, and moral principles, at times our behavior can be better understood as more base displays of territoriality; unwitting biological patterns; and aggressive, animal imperatives. Often we act like the animals we are. In many instances our only significantly "higher" human expressions consist of the ways in which we hide or explain away our base instincts.

Often conversation is only a way of avoiding murdering one another. Less intense examples are commonplace. When a guest visits and later leaves the home territory of friends or acquaintances, not even the most welcome ones can come and go without ceremony unless there is an established level of easy intimacy that allows exceptions to the rules. Even invited guests must knock and be admitted. Faced with the disturbed instinctual protective responses to this encounter, greetings are demanded in which eye contact, facial expression, and conventional verbal exchanges assure both parties that there is no danger in their coming together; home territory cannot be violated.

The desert greeting *shalom* translates as the assurance of "peace." Whether by handshake or by waving "Hi," exposure of the empty, unclenched hand shows that no weapon is being carried. Even in the "civilized" suburbs of America, both the visitor and those who are visited quickly make clear that they are very glad to see each other, assuring one another that they mean no harm. The hosts offer ritual gifts of food or drink to show that they do not fear that the other has come to take these things. The visitor is expected to accept the gifts and so assure the host that this token will suffice as a safeguard against the guest not taking everything else. Only after these ceremonial assurances have been transacted can friends settle into a series of more casually comfortable exchanges.

Sometime later in the visit there is another shift. Spontaneously the frequency of positive statements increases with densely repeated expression of good feelings about hospitality, ease and enjoyment of having been together, and promises to meet again very soon. These include statements such as, "It's really been a good evening," "I enjoyed being in touch with you," "We need to do this more often," and "Be sure to stay in touch."

It becomes clear to everyone that the evening is coming to a close. These deferential gestures are ways of ameliorating the implied offense of abandonment inherent in leaving or being left. As the guest begins to leave, these expressions and gestures become more intense and more frequent, often ending with an assuring embrace. Usually people do not leave quickly. The hosts also participate in slowing the leaving into a gradual transition. Even though everyone has decided that the evening is over, some time must be spent standing around in final exchange. This gets carried out until everyone feels comfortable enough with the leaving to be assured that their instinctually antisocial impulses are sufficiently suppressed.

Should the embarrassment of a replay occur, the whole transaction is exposed as having been something of a sham. For example, even in a warm, wonderful parting of good friends, happy to see each other and sad to separate again, if once outside on the walk the guests discover that one of them has left behind a scarf or gloves, there is an uncomfortably awkward feeling at having to return.

Once back on the porch, the returning guests are hesitant to knock. Behind the closed door, the host and hostess exchange a grimace of irritation, as if to say, "What the hell are they doing back?" Muted expressions of dismay are constrained to uneasy glances or questioning shrugs. The door is opened. Apologizing for having left the scarf, the guests come back in.

At this point any renewed exchange of how good it was to be together will be forced and fragmented, aborted lest its insincerity be too obvious. The disruptive quality of the unplanned return gives the lie to the good feelings expressed at the first leave-taking.

In conventional social situations most of us tend to make small talk as a way of gradually easing into intimacy. We assure each other of our interest, concern, and good intentions by saying, "Glad to see you," "How are you?," and the like. As a therapist I do none of this in meeting with a patient.

Early in the therapy the patient may attempt deferential social gestures as a carry-over from the conventional manner of relating. Soon this gives way to talking about whatever is really on one's mind from the start. If not, I confront this defensive behavior as a maneuver meant to avoid more troublesome matters, or as an attempt to control the therapy by insisting that I react with reciprocal deference.

From the very beginning, the patient was faced with unexpected ambiguities that resisted resolution into familiar social categories. My style of meeting was largely free of the ceremonial lubricants used to ease ordinary social interactions. Wherever possible I avoided the ritualized manners that so often afford the appearance of civility concocted to contain unguarded personal encounter. My pointed refusal to provide remedial gloss or personal relief at that time increased the patient's level of uncertainty and anxiety. This raised the risk that the patient might leave. At the same time it demanded that, should the patient stay, he or she would have to deal more deeply and openly with his or her disruptive underlying passions.

The process began with the prospective patient's initial attempt to contact me. When someone calls my office, the phone does not ring. A light that only I can see blinks to let me know there will be a message for me at my switchboard in the lobby. This allows ongoing therapy sessions to go undisturbed. The switchboard operator is instructed to ring through only if there is an urgent call from my wife or from one of my kids. There are no other emergencies in my profession.

Picking up my phone messages at the switchboard allows me to choose which ones I answer. I do not open all my mail and see no reason to be any more a prisoner of the phone company than of the postal service. Typically the phone message reads, "Mrs. Mary Smith called to request a therapy appointment," followed by her phone number.

At my convenience, I call back, saying, "Mary Smith, this is Sheldon Kopp." This immediately takes the first contact out of the traditional doctor-patient mode, posing us as social peers, leaving the relationship undefined, and requiring a conscious choice of salutation by the patient. If I have free time, I meet the patient's request for an initial appointment with encouragement that we get together to see if we like each other well enough to work together. I offer a time, a firm offer without accommodation. If the patient balks about its inconvenience (many do), I am ready to recommend another therapist. Most callers find a way to work out being able to accept the hour I offer, and so we resolve initial demand for ceremonial accommodation on my part.

I am quite serious about our choosing each other. During that first hour we must get to know each other a bit. I do *not* assume in advance that the patient will choose to work with me. I always ask how the patient feels about being with me to allow consideration of not coming back. In turn, I, too, was shopping for someone to work with who would be of interest to me. Somewhere, late in the first hour, I will respond by stating whether or not I am willing to work with the patient. To increase my own freedom in this regard, I let the patient know that unless we both agree to work together, there will be no charge for that initial consultation .

In dealing with reluctant patients with whom I am willing to work, my Shiva stance was to raise the ante.

If he or she resisted my contract stipulations, I increased the demands. If a patient insisted on uncertainty about whether or not to come as often as once a week, I would insist that to work with me, he or she would have to come twice a week. If a patient felt that he or she might like to try treatment for a couple of weeks just to see how it worked out, I insisted on a three-month commitment. If the patient was unwilling to agree, it was fine with me that we not go on. I made it even harder for the reluctant patient to return by insisting that if he or she never called me again I would not charge for the initial consultation. By simply not getting in touch with me, the patient could save that money, retaining without charge whatever was gained from that first hour. Should the patient decide to come back in the future ready to meet my contract demands, then I would charge for the initial consultation as well.

One problem that arose in power plays with resistant patients was the issue of good faith. The patient might agree to a three-month, twice-a-week trial period of psychotherapy but might have lurking in back of his or her mind the strategy of dropping out earlier without my being able to do anything about the reneging. In some cases I resolved this power struggle by insisting on a cash retainer. The patient might well feel suspicious that I would somehow push him or her into breaking the contract so I could keep the unearned money. To set such a patient in a disruptive double bind, I defined the retainer if the contract was broken as money that the patient would lose but that I would *not* gain. For example, one such patient was a Jewish man in passive marital struggles over religious differences with his Catholic wife. He was unwilling to make a commitment. I insisted on a retainer of two hundred dollars in the form of a check made out to Catholic Charities, payable only if he broke the contract.

Once the contract is in place, each session begins exactly at the appointed time. I enter the waiting room, make momentary eye contact, and greet the patient with an invitation that is some simple variant of, "You can come on in now." The patient follows me into my office. Until the patient begins to speak, I am silent and make no further eye contact. As the patient enters and leaves my office, I open and close the door. This is one of the ways in which I define myself as guardian of the gate and keeper of the beginnings and endings of our time together.

After closing the door, I cross the room and take my usual seat. Once seated, I neither speak nor do I look up until the patient has begun to speak. Instead, I sit with my eyes closed in Shiva-like Yoga posture, concentrating on my breathing. This may last anywhere from a few seconds to several minutes. My avoidance of eye contact eliminates our participating in any nonverbal deferential ceremonial or social gestures, leaving the patient free to get in touch with what is going on inside at that moment.

When the patient does speak, my uncluttered attention is alert both to the content and the tone of what is expressed. (Should the patient's silence go on much longer than usual, I may look up, and respond to any remarkable nonverbal behavior as the first communication of the session.)

By beginning each therapy session with my silence, I express my trust that though the patient may not believe it, he or she knows best where to begin. Should the patient choose to wait for me to initiate our exchange, the first thing likely to be expressed in our fifty-minute meeting is my saying, "Our time is up for today."

Patients tend to respond on a number of different levels to my initial silence and inwardness. These often follow a definite progression. Early in our work together, any patient who is uneasy about anticipated rejection often experiences my opening posture as disinterest or aloofness. Eventually my behavior communicates the implicit message, "I am here. There are no demands on you." Eventually many patients come to feel relieved to experience so open a break in the circle of time that no external expectations need be met. It allows the patient to pay attention to what is going on within.

Should the patient begin with an attempt at amenities, such as asking me, "How are you today?," it is unlikely that I will answer at all. If I acknowledge the overture (because it persists), it is likely that I will do so by wondering aloud, "What do you suppose you are up to?" or by interpreting the patient's behavior as a devious distraction, a desperate stalling maneuver, a shallow attempt at bribery, or some other tactic that that particular patient typically uses as a character defense against anxiety. Or if the patient is sufficiently stubborn and I am feeling particularly playful that day, I may acquiesce by offering an incredibly detailed description of the state of my health, going on and on until in despair the patient interrupts.

Contrasted with the seeming continuity of ordinary everyday social interactions, these therapeutic disruptions cast the patient into a kaleidoscopically lunatic perspective akin to Alice's Wonderland. The topsy-turvy quality of the Shiva stance is one in which the therapist is always one up on the patient. The reciprocity of their superior and inferior positions is maintained both crudely by the patient's defensive demands and subtly by the therapist's technical maneuvers. The disarming interplay is one in which the patient insists overtly that I am directing the process while he or she desperately tries to take covert control of the session. I in turn insist that I am in charge of the therapy to help the patient accept authority over his or her life.

At the outset the patient submits to this uneasy balance by coming voluntarily to seek my help, by seeing me at my convenience, and by paying me a great deal of money. He or she is to say whatever comes to mind without regard to standards of what is rational, appropriate, or socially decent. I need say nothing, and often I do just that. We act as if often the patient will not know what he or she is *really* trying to say because of underlying unconscious motives. I, on the other hand, am assumed to be an expert about such matters. My reactions to the patient's behavior are "interpretations," while the patient's evaluations of my attitudes are "fantasies."

But whenever the patient accepts that I am there as a technical consultant, I may insist that he or she must consider my feelings to be those of just another struggling human being. Paradoxically, I am also the detached expert just doing my job and unconcerned about the patient getting better. At the same time, I am there as a caring person who offers what help he can but who knows no more about how people ought to live than the patient does.

The apparent perversity of my shifting attitudes has a hidden meaning that would lose its value if directly revealed to the patient. The therapeutic judo of my tactics is aimed at the interruption of both the patient's self-restricting, risk-avoiding character defenses, and of the face-saving gloss of his or her mannered social interactions. My shift to being present as another vulnerable human being who is there to tell his own tale reflects my willingness to be a companion to the patient in the chaos that follows these interruptions. I may spin the patient around and turn him or her upside down, but when the patient comes down in the rubble of life, I will be there as a committed though world-weary companion. And as the patient undertakes the frightening pilgrimage of a life open to the perils of the dark forces from which he or she would usually hide, I will be found alongside, hoping that we may draw courage from one another. My telling the patient all of this in advance would be futile. I would not be believed. Why should the patient come to trust me until he or she comes to know me? Even if the patient would blindly follow my instructions in hope of getting what he or she came for, those efforts would lack the spontaneous vitality of unplanned actions arising in the fire of the moment.

Gradually this disruption of directed dialogue can help the patient to know that he or she is to be trusted. In part, it contains my tacit communication: "This is *your* time to get to experience what is going on inside you. You know best. Wherever you wish to begin must be exactly the right place for you right now." Much to the patient's surprise, he or she must lead in this self-examination. I guide along the way by following wherever the patient would go. Like the uneasy encounter of animals in a forest, the meetings and partings of people in less primitive places are highly sensitized interactions. The entering and leaving of one another's space always involves some instinctual territorial response of invasion or of being invaded, and of abandonment or of being abandoned. Because of the implied instinctual threat, deferential gestures are required to quiet the powerful internal forces that are stirred by these disruptions.

Upset by my not being "nice and polite," the patient might experience me as cold, callous, brutal, and perverse. At the same time I remain responsible for remembering that whatever the unceremonial nature of psychotherapy, patient and therapist are social beings operating within a culturally sanctioned context, fulfilling an economic contract. Our basic *therapeutic alliance* involves an agreement to work together at a specified time and place; our mutual task is to help the patient to be happier. The therapist is a professional who exchanges expert services for money; the patient is a client who pays for help.

If our time together is to prove useful, we must establish a therapeutic alliance that engenders enough trust to open the opportunity for the patient to uncover unconscious passions previously put aside. But in addition to that easy alliance, the harsh-seeming disruption of a *therapeutic barrier* must also be put in place. This transforming barrier appears as the therapist's arbitrary prerogative to act at any point *as if* the situation were not real. The patient and I meet in alliance as any two free agents might, talking out his or her problems *between* us. But anywhere along the way, I may raise the barrier by shifting the focus onto the *way* in which the patient is discussing the matter, saying, "You reacted as if I were your critical father (or mother, brother, etc.)."

At one level this interruptive shift is an interpretation of the transference—that is, a focusing of the patient's tension on the old unresolved feelings that influence his or her current behavior and that in this instance have been transferred onto the person of the therapist. But more important, this raising of the therapeutic barrier is one of the many ways in which the therapist under-

mines the social reality, making the patient more vulnerable to the dark forces that churn beneath the surface
and open us unexpectedly to intense interruption of the
surface logic and order of what is being presented. The
constancy of the content is shattered by the changing
shift to focusing on the form.

I began by ignoring the *content* of the patient's complaints, focusing instead entirely on the *style* in which
the material is presented. Or alternately, in individual
therapy I might get the patient to focus on past history.
In group therapy I encouraged the patient's curiosity
about the group process. Some of what occurred as the
patient reluctantly took on these tasks was induction of
an experience of loss of a self now given over to the assigned work. Immersion in this new task disrupted the
patient's willful self-sorry attachment to getting immediate sympathy and relief from every appointed caretaker in the vicinity. Instead, a new possibility arose:
The patient could begin to experience the therapist and
the other group members as real people with souls of
their own, as people who had a meaning outside the
patient's self-preoccupation. This allows them to become significant others who then can put the patient in
touch with the meaning of his or her own life.

At the time of my honoring Shiva as a therapist, I
instructed only by indirection. My tactical rule of thumb
for meeting patients was, *"Be where they ain't!"* Within
the perverse guidelines of this interruptive instruction,
the patient who began with immersion in his or her own
history was drawn back again and again to what was
going on in the here and now. The hysterically emotional, overly impulsive patient was slowed down to
stop and think about what he or she was doing. The
obsessionally paralyzed thinker was met with responses
so irrational that emotional upset made it impossible to

hold back any longer. Patients who were initially too hard on themselves were treated gently and indulgently. Self-sorry whiners were confronted with demands so harsh that no quarter was left for excuse-making. To those who demanded clarity, I spoke metaphorically. Only those who kept things muddled evoked my direct confrontation.

A clear example of how outrageously interruptive I was willing to be during that Kali Yuga of my professional life occurred in a psychotherapy group. The meeting began in the usual mode of a brief initial silence followed by each of us doing his or her number. Melvin was stickily preoccupied with his plight, luxuriating in his usual low-keyed anguish of obsession over all his inadequacies. "It's just no use at all," he said, whining. "Months and months of therapy, and still I'm never really myself." I pointed out that the one problem nobody could possibly have was not being himself or herself.

Melvin seemed pleased with the opportunity to go on and explain, to go on and on and on. He described at length how he could not be spontaneous, could not get past his hung-up expectation of acting inadequately. He insisted that he was unable to respond in the here and now. I offered to help then and there. If he would trust me for a moment, I would teach him to trust himself by letting him experience the here and now, spontaneously and competently. Offered the opportunity to solve his problems, Melvin was understandably reluctant. He eyed me suspiciously but responded to group pressure at least to try to trust me.

During this exchange I was holding a lit cigar. The moment Melvin agreed to trust me, I flipped the smoking butt across the room straight into his lap. Suddenly his whiningly lethargic, gelatinous manner gave way to

alert and angry action as he expertly fielded the hot
cigar, shouted, "Goddamn you anyway, Kopp!," and
tossed it back at me with verve and accuracy.

His eyes were wide with wonder and vitality. Uncharacteristically he announced, "I've got some other
unfinished business to take care of in this group right
now." He blurted out some long-withheld anger toward
one of the other men in the group and then told one of
the women how much he cared about her. Crossing the
room with clear purpose, he hugged her with unrestrained tenderness.

In the midst of the embrace, Melvin began to mutter
something about how he might mess this up. The group
told him to shut up and enjoy himself. He seemed
pleased to surrender to the moment once more.

Having since become conscious of Krishna, it is with
some embarrassment that I offer this account of my
savagely Shiva-like, outrageously intrusive behavior. The
fact that at the time it worked well no longer seems
adequate justification for maintaining my earlier assaul-
tive Kali attitude of unalleviated therapeutic disruption.

Chapter 7

The Many Faces of Love

Easy times are sweet. Hard times are bitter. Bittersweet mixtures of the two are experienced intermittently by everyone. As times change, the next necessity in our ever-shifting situation invites the intervention of yet another god. The Hindu pantheon provides. When all again is lost to Shiva/Kali, once more Brahma, the Creator, awakens to fill the void by redividing himself into a newly created universe.

For a while, the living is easy. As in any coming together of complementary parts or well-matched people, inevitably all too soon comes the souring of the honeymoon sweetness. Elements enter into opposition as initial idealized commitments weaken and deterioration of harmony begins. It is then that the Sustainer and Preserver of the Universe, manifests his concern by reappearing to restore order and well-being.

In one of his many manifestations, large, swift, and wide-striding, Vishnu arrives to fulfill his commitment to save humans from needless suffering. On the back of his sacred eagle, Garuda, the Preserver joyfully descends from the luminous sky to declare his dedication to rescuing us from the demonic darkness into which we have begun to fall. Whatever his manifestation of the moment, we can always depend on Vishnu's devotion. Symbolically implemented by the treasures of his magic powers, in his expansive, caring hands he brings the gifts of the mace that enforces the will of the human spirit, the conch shell that endows the necessary skills for achieving its purposes, the lotus that engenders the love that sustains us throughout our suffering, and the disc of discernment that brings the wisdom necessary for reordering our priorities.

In Hindu mythology, Vishnu descends to earth to defeat the demonic forces that disrupt the moral order and easy living. At times, the demons represent the dark, personally unloving aspects of our attitudes and actions toward each other that evoke unnecessary human suffering. Mainly they simply stand for the random calamities that life impersonally imposes as indifferent necessities of misfortune marked "To whom it may concern."

As preserver of moral order, Vishnu comes to protect our physical and emotional well-being. Ever ready to offer himself in opposition to the demons, he is eternally on call to rescue those whose welfare he cherishes.

The variety of his incarnations is as infinite as the time cycles to which each corresponds. Each avatar of Vishnu is an illusory manifestation of only one aspect of all that love can be. The form that Vishnu takes at any given time is determined by the needs of those to whose welfare he is devoted. His ever-changing incarnations are not expressions of his own needs, but of his response to the neediness of those he loves.

Over the centuries, the evolving images of Vishnu found in Hindu writings start, stop, and shift. In the later popular legends,[1] his devotees conventionalize the lore of the Preserver into a litany of only ten incarnations. The first five are mythological, the next three heroic. The ninth appears to be an attempt to assimilate the growing popularity of Buddhism into an advanced form of Vishnu worship, and the tenth is an eschatological anticipation of salvation yet to come.

The earliest incarnations of these ten appear in the shape of animals. Even so, the love they bring is no less than that which will come later in his more human manifestations. The first was Matsya, the fish. During a deluge, the demons stole the holy writings. Vishnu appeared in the form of a fish to rescue the Hindu Noah, Manu, from the flood. Vishnu restored the moral order by instructing Manu in teachings of the stolen Vedas.

During the chaos following the flood, Vishnu reappeared in his second incarnation as Kurma, the tortoise. It was a time when gods could still make foolish mistakes, show weakness, and lose battles. Freer from error, certain spiritually developed human beings were sometimes powerful enough to best the gods in the sort of struggles in which human beings today imagine themselves inevitably doomed to defeat.

During that time, the king of the gods offended a spiritually dedicated seer who was fulfilling a vow of devotion. Infuriated by the impulsive irreverence of Indra's arrogant interruption, the sage cursed the king of the gods and his retinue to an era miserably marred by misfortune. His curse robbed the gods of the vitality that came from drinking the ambrosia of immortality. The sacred chalice containing that liquid of love was thrown by the sage to the bottom of the sea of milk.

In their time of desperation, as always the gods turned to Vishnu for help. He advised them to enter into an alliance with the demons, promising that together they could churn the sea of milk until it returned the liquid of immortality and other wonderful gifts as well. Vishnu assured the gods that he would see to it that the demons would not get any undeserved share of the treasured nectar.

Under Vishnu's instruction the gods and the demons cooperated in combining the mountain of Mandara as a staff and the serpent Vasuki as a cord into an instrument to churn the milky ocean. The spinning mountain began to bore into the earth and threatened to destroy it. Vishnu saved the world by assuming the form of a gigantic turtle whose shell served as a protective pivot against any damage that might be done by the whirling Mount Mandara.

A second threat was posed by the pained reaction of the serpent who served as the churning cord. With its tail pulled by the gods and its head by the demons, the snake spat out torrents of venom that threatened to destroy all living things. Vishnu called on the god Shiva to drink the poison. Since that time Shiva has borne a blue mark on his throat as an emblematic scar of his having helped Vishnu to save the world from destruction.[2]

In time, the combined churning efforts of the gods and the demons were rewarded by the appearance of a miraculously nurturing cow, an intoxicating wine goddess, by heavenly tree nymphs who perfumed the flowers of the earth, and by many other wondrous delights. Eventually even the radiant Sri emerged. The holy water of the Ganges was poured upon this long-awaited beautiful goddess of prosperity by the sacred elephants whose pillars support the universe, sanctifying Sri as Vishnu's devoted wife. In addition to the reappearance of Sri (later known as Lakshimi, the goddess of fortune), the bounty of Vishnu's beneficence yielded up the healing system of medicine, the miraculous horse, the moon that Shiva was to wear upon his forehead, and many other gracious gifts.

Finally, the spirit of healing himself arose from the sea of milk, holding high in his upraised hand the cup containing the liquid of immortality. But before the gods could drink the nectar, the demons snatched it away and fled.

Once again Vishnu interceded. Assuming a fascinating female form, he seduced the demons with illusion. As they argued over who would possess this irresistible female, Vishnu recaptured the nectar and returned it to the gods. Quickly drinking down the magical ambrosia, they regained their vitality and used their renewed power to drive away the demons. Like the generations of humans he had earlier saved, the gods themselves were gratefully devoted to Vishnu.

During a subsequent cycle, the demon king Hiranyaksha dragged the earth down to the bottom of the sea. Vishnu, the rescuer, reappeared once more. This time as Vahara, the wild cosmic boar, he descended to the ocean bottom, tracked down the scent of the lost land, defeated the demons, and returned to the sea's surface with the earth hooked on to his long, curved, sharp tusks.

In the cycle following Vishnu's slaying of Hiranyaksha, the throne of the king of demons was filled by his twin brother, Hiranyaksasipu. The new demon king's reign threatened every living creature. Because he lived under a spell that protected him from being killed "by man or beast," he could not be defeated. Out of continuing concern for the welfare of the universe, Vishnu returned in the avatar of Narashima, a man-lion. His composite form imaginatively evaded the protective prophecy under which the demon endured, allowing Vishnu to destroy him.

That fourth incarnation introduces a partially human aspect to Vishnu's varying forms. His fifth avatar as

Vamana, the dwarf, makes him even more unmistakably human though not yet the epitome of that incarnation.

During a Treta Yuga (the third throw of the cosmic dice), in his dwarf form, Vishnu challenged the demon Bali's new cruel domination of the three worlds of heaven, earth, and hell. The god of preservation went to the sacred place where Bali was making a sacrifice. Pretending to honor the demon king of the triple world, Vamana begged to be allowed one small favor. He asked only that Bali grant him whatever space he could cover in three strides. Viewing the tiny supplicant with contempt, the demon king agreed. Vishnu then expanded into his true divine proportions, appearing openly as the great giant of the universe. His eyes became the moon and the sun, his feet the earth, and his head the sky. In two great strides, he covered and reclaimed both heaven and earth. Foregoing the third step, he left the underworld to Bali and banished all the demons back to hell.

The avatars of Vishnu continued to evolve into more and more human form. After the first three animal aspects as fish, tortoise, and boar, he appeared as the composite man/beast, and then as the dwarf/giant. Vishnu's later incarnations became increasingly human until in Oriental equivalent of Jesus, he was idealized into the most human form of the gods' sacrifice, devotion, and redemptive love.

Like the cycle of time itself, the legendary avatar evolution is a gradual and disrupted broken circle. Following the dwarf, Vamana, comes Rama with the axe, attacking the tyranny of the antagonistic members of the Kshatriya warrior-politician caste. Originally overlord of this caste, Arjuna's invincible strength and endurance were enhanced by magic powers of shape-shifting. But Arjuna had made the mistake of coveting and capturing the sacrificial cow and a calf of a certain saintly sage.

To redeem the bovine symbols of nurturant love, Vishnu appeared in the form of Rama, son of the victimized sage. Filled with fury, battle-ax in hand, he pursued Arjuna and his army. Single-handedly, Rama destroyed the tyrant along with his warriors, elephants, and chariots.

Arjuna took up five hundred bows and arrows in his thousand arms. Rama axed them all in a single blow. Rescuing cow and calf, he returned them to his father. Once the battles were won, Rama relinquished his weapon, composed his heart and mind, and watched over the good people of the earth throughout the remainder of that time cycle.

In his seventh avatar, Vishnu appeared once again as a second Rama. He had by then evolved beyond the status of a simple heroic warrior. In this incarnation as the devoted Rama of the epic *Ramayana*,[3] he offered a model of selfless service to easing the suffering of fellow beings.

Even in this incarnation there is still the self-aggrandizing heroic exploit of slaying the powerful demon king Ravana. But much of Rama's service to his family and to his people came in the form of more modest self-sacrifice.

Needing less to be the personal pivot of good works, in this incarnation Vishnu depended on other embodiments of the pursuit of pure service to others. At this point in time the worship of Vishnu moved toward its apogee of devotion in the ultimate avatar of Krishna (whose sweet appeal will be detailed in the chapter that follows). Eventually, as his ninth avatar, even the compassionate Buddha was claimed by the worshipers of Vishnu. In this Christ-like aspect as the Bodhisattva, before he himself entered the ecstasy of Nirvana, Buddha delayed his own release from suffering to devote himself to helping every other sentient being's release.

According to Vishnu's devotees, the tenth avatar is yet to come. As Kalki, the next lord of creation, he will reappear riding a white steed to rescue us all from the moral and physical decay of the present Kali Yuga. Renovating our disordered world and restoring our lost purity, this Messiah of the present age will challenge the forces of time itself. Unloading the dice of necessity, he will allow even the Kali era to become a golden age, awakening us to a bright new day at the end of a long dark night.

In fulfilling my own commitments as husband/father to family and as psychotherapist to patients, for most of my adult life it has been easier for me to identify with the earlier, more primitive archetypal avatars of Vishnu than with the sweeter, softer aspects of his later incarnations. Interlaced with traditional male cultural values, my own mock-heroic personality defenses strongly supported my standing as sustainer of the universe in postures such as unfailing provider, acknowledged patriarch, and authoritarian problem-solver.

Clearly I was then closer to possession by the benevolently terrible god Shiva, the Destroyer, than to devotion to the lovingly sublime Vishnu, the Preserver. My earlier efforts at rescuing loved ones for whom I felt responsible might have been more rightly represented metaphorically by the unrelenting and ferocious wielding of the sword of necessary justice commanded by Shiva's consort Kali. Only lately can I envision my efforts as merciful melodies prettily played on Krishna's flute.

My intuitive introversive psychological temperament allowed easy identification with Shiva's high-minded, ascetically principled elevation above passion. Krishna's simpler pedestrian devotion to playful personal contact does not come to me as easily. I do not mean to exaggerate the earlier imbalance to imply that I was no more than an impersonally dogged disciplinarian, never lovingly playful, indulgently emphatic, nor ever beyond the bounds of Stoic self-seriousness. Nonetheless, though alternately enthralled by each of the gods, for a period in the past pervasive enough to warrant my retrospective regret I certainly was more subject to Shiva than is comfortable in my current commitment to Krishna.

Aging and invalidism have combined to restrain my earlier shamelessly Shiva-like stance. Softened by restricted energies and abilities that require my depending more on the efforts of others, and offered opportunities expanded by the women and children newly entering my family, I am trying to transform my inflated independence into Krishna's sweeter style of embrace. Hopefully this will save me from becoming stuck in the aging hero's role of the crotchety, crippled tyrant.

As in all such conversions from the auspices of one god to another, unexpectedly I have encountered unimagined epiphanies. Turning as I did from the ascetic yogin god Shiva to the more pastoral, people-conscious Krishna aspect of the god Vishnu, I imagined that I was only entering the unknown extroverted aspects of my personality. I was not surprised, then, that many dreams reflected otherwise ignored avenues of interpersonal relations such as socializing, attention-attracting displays, personal ambition, material acquisition, and the like.

I should know by now that every time I innocently imagine that I can turn a corner without running into the unexpected, I get knocked on my ass. Each time eventually I pick myself up, brush myself off, and get on with it. Only then do I find myself rewarded by whatever previously undiscovered treasures occur beyond the unexpected obstacles. Again and again I recommit myself to future explorations, certain that next time I will remember to expect the unexpected and to anticipate the surprises. I never do.

This time the first unexpected encounter came in the form of a dream. The "facts" of my life were challenged by the dream images. In my daytime waking life, I have been the only son of a long-dead mother and father whose only marriage was to each other. Psychologically, I was mainly my Kali mother's son, aggressively acting out a ruthlessly tough self-seeking stance. Though she accused me of being an outlaw, I was her warrior. My Krishna father was the more traditionally maternal of the two parents. He was a softly passive, playfully receptive, and sweetly giving, easy sort of man. Uncharacteristically, about once a year he would come home from his daily underground trek to the office, having punched out an enemy encountered on the subway. His unfortunate episodic violence was always explained as a situational slip that was both unaccountable and insignificant.

In this transformation dream, when I came upon him on the platform of a New York subway, my dead father was alive and well. Amiable as usual, he greeted me warmly and invited me to come along to meet someone. Though I could not remember having met him before, the young man to whom he introduced me seemed familiar. My father told me that this would be my last chance to meet this man because he was awaiting execution for murder. He introduced the stranger as his son from a previous marriage.

Waking from the dream, I immediately understood that this was the first of a series of dreams that was yet to be completed. I knew this because I felt no emotional response to this remarkable dream. Instead, all I experienced was the overwhelming astonishment of a cognitive collision with this totally unexpected retelling of my life history.

I understood that my shift from Kali to Krishna meant not only a new god but also a reincarnated identity. I was to complete my family legacy by transformation from being my mother's son to becoming my father's son. This disruption would require recognition of the destructive aspects of my earlier lifelong posture and death of my earlier self-centered conceit.

Later I retold the dream to someone close to me. Suddenly I saw that not only was I to shift in this cycle from the psychological son of my Shiva/Kali mother to that of my Vishnu/Krishna father. Additionally I was to be the new wife in my father's second marriage. It was tempting to imagine this as upsetting only because of the implied homosexual incestuous features of the transformation. In my heart I knew that something far more awesome was occurring. I had encountered the death of one self-image and the transformed identity of another. The dream announced encounter with another aspect of my self, a future to be fulfilled by facing another of the gods.

NOTES

1. In the Puranas (3300 B.C. through A.D. 1500).

2. As occasionally opposing but ultimately united aspects of the universal soul, Vishnu and Shiva appear together in some of the Hindu myths

either in competition or in cooperation with
one another.

3. *Ramayana: King Rama's Way*, Valmiki's *Ramayana* told
in English prose by William Buck (New
York: New American Library, 1978).

Chapter 8

Becoming Conscious of Krishna

Of the many faces of Vishnu's love, it is his eighth avatar that presently mirrors my own image. More and more, I become conscious of Krishna. Commitment to that god compels growing awareness of my own Krishna character.

Throughout the many popular legends[1] of his dedicated devotion to the simple people who depended upon him, the beloved blue-black boy-man perennially maintained his youthfully mischievous playfulness. Appealing more and more to each new generation of Hindus, Krishna has become the most celebrated hero of Indian mythology. His origins have taken on the classic characteristics of many mythic culture heroes. He is understood to be a divine offering in human form sent to save simple souls from needless suffering. Like other menaced messiahs, before birth he was threatened by the promised slaughter of innocents. To avoid annihilation, he was a king disguised as a commoner, a deceptive device that mirrored his manifestation as a god masquerading as a mortal. This deception required his being raised incognito by foster parents who did not know that he was a divine child.

In the myth of Krishna, it was King Kamsa who

assailed the innocent infants. At the wedding of his cousin Devaki to her bridegroom, Vasudeva, a voice from the heavens warned the cruel king that someday he would be killed by her eighth embryo. In typically mythic irony, his futile attempt to preempt the prophecy facilitated its fulfillment.

Kamsa was about to kill his cousin when her husband implored that she be spared. Vasudeva promised to surrender each infant arising out of his wife's womb. Accepting this assurance, Kamsa let Devaki live but held the couple in house arrest.

At the same time that this mortal drama was unfolding, the goddess Earth went to the gods seeking a savior from an era of ever-increasing swarms of demons. Vishnu agreed to intercede. Pulling one white and one black hair from his head, he provided these portions of himself to descend to earth to eliminate the evolving evil. This sacrifice would destroy Kamsa, king of the demonic forces. The Preserver promised that these hairs would appear as the seventh and eighth embryos in the womb of the divine Devaki.

Six sons of Vishnu already existed as demons in the underworld.[2] One at a time, Vishnu set his sons in Devaki's womb. At birth each was delivered to Kamsa by Vasudeva. One by one the king killed these children. Embedded as an infinitesimal portion of Vishnu, the seventh child was made to appear to have been miscarried, aborted by Devaki's fear of Kamsa's wrath. At that point, as promised, Vishnu himself took on an embryonic human aspect in the holy womb of Devaki. Born as her eighth child, Vishnu evolved in her body in the form of the baby Krishna.

On the dark night of Krishna's birth, Kamsa's guards were made heavy with sleep. Instructed by Vishnu,

Vasudeva took the infant Krishna to the home of the couple who were to be his foster parents.

Impregnated earlier with the white hair of Vishnu, Yasoda, wife of the cowherd Nanda, had already borne a son named Balarama. In the darkness of this fateful night, Yasoda gave birth to a daughter. Stealing secretly into the home of the foster parents, Vasudeva replaced the newborn baby girl in Yasoda's bed with the boy child Krishna and delivered the daughter to Devaki's bed. In the early morning light, Yasoda was ecstatic to discover that her new child was a son who, in fitting contrast to his pure white foster brother Balarama, was dark as a blue lotus petal.

When Kamsa discovered the girl child in Devaki's bed, he seized the infant by the foot, whirled her around his head, and dashed her to death on the stone floor. Instantly transformed, the little girl arose into the sky as the goddess Devi. She called down to the king that the one who would destroy him had now been born. Kamsa trembled with fear and rage.

Because things had been going badly on earth, the lord Vishnu had once again allowed himself to be born into the world of people. To restore their easy living, he returned to rid the earth of those demons in human form who appear as kings that abuse their power. For the good of humankind, he was born the son of the princess Devaki and raised as the foster child of the cowherds Yasoda and Nanda. Living as Krishna for one hundred twenty-five years, he came carrying the four power gifts in his four hands, ready at birth to begin fulfillment of his mission on earth. The changes he was to institute began when Devi shamed Kamsa from the sky, filling the demon king with remorse sufficient to move him to free Vasudeva and Devaki from the house arrest under which he had held them.

Living as the child of poor cowherds, immediately the baby began righting wrongs. The infant Krishna demonstrated his power by overthrowing a cart, pulling up trees by the roots, and otherwise manifesting his potential power for resolving the problems in the village.

Even as an infant, Krishna was able to eradicate evil. In this incarnation the earliest instance was his encounter with Putana, the demonic child-killer who destroyed babies by giving them suck from her poisonous breasts. One night she made the mistake of attempting her awful attack on the sleeping Krishna. Grabbing her nipple, he sucked out her poisoned milk and her life along with it. Armed with the disc of discernment, he had penetrated her nourishing-mother disguise to reveal the hideously putrid sorceress hidden beneath. Investing her reversal of poison posed as milk, the baby Krishna was able to turn the course of her noxious nursing from endangering him to destroying her.

Reversal is only one of his ruses. Another is that of *concealment*, in which everyday details mask the majesty of greater dimensions of devotion in the expansive spirit hidden within the small gesture.

Early examples include Kirshna pretending to be a good boy while secretly doing naughty things. Even his mischief was a source of secret pleasure to those he loved. Krishna and his brother Balarama were forever crawling through the mud and playing boyish pranks that affectionately aggravated the cowherd women. Teasingly the boys would set loose calves, steal candy to eat, and distribute food to the monkeys. Their apparently aggravating antics served to amuse and distract the women from the drudgery of daily chores.

One day, the other children told Krishna's foster mother Yasoda that he had eaten dirt. The scolded Krishna pleaded that she look into his mouth to see that they were lying. When Krishna opened wide his mouth, Yasoda was astonished to discover that it contained the entire eternal universe. Seeing within her baby the miniature mountains, oceans, islands, wind, and water, as well as the moon and the stars, she imagined herself deluded. Once she realized that this baby held a heavenly refuge, her mind and heart were eased. At that point, Krishna once again inverted her illusion into the form of her maternal affection. In an instant, Yasoda could no longer remember what she had seen. Instead, her mother's heart filled with love as she became aware only that her beautiful blue baby was innocent of having eaten dirt. All that she could feel was that he was fine, she was fine, and their being together was finer yet.

As an early adolescent, Krishna expanded his adventuresome *inversion of opposites*, this time into the counterpoints of poison and ambrosia. Vishnu's sleeping on the serpent of eternity from which he awakened to ride on the glorious Garuda bird had already prefigured these polarities. As an adolescent, Krishna encountered the negative aspect of the sacred serpent in the form of Kaliya, the snake who poisoned the pools of the cowherds. Until Krishna appeared, so that they would be spared their venom, the cowherds had felt obligated at the beginning of each month to make offerings to the serpents. Kaliya was a particularly arrogant serpent who accepted the offerings without reciprocating. As a bird symbolizing the egg of birth, Garuda had been sent by Vishnu to punish the poisonous snake. In ambush, the serpentine symbol of death hid at the bottom of the pool where Garuda came to eat fish, poisoning the pond while waiting secretly to destroy the sweet bird of life.

One hot summer day, in their thirst, some of the cowherds and their cows drank from the polluted pool.

When young Krishna came along, he found them life-
less on the bank. Climbing a high tree, the youth plunged
into the poisoned water. Sensing the swirl set up by the
strenuous swimming, Kaliya rose to the surface, catch-
ing Krishna in his coils. When the rest of the cowherds
came along looking for Krishna, they were terrified that
he would be destroyed by the serpent. Had the gods
not intervened to stop them, the cowherds would have
entered the pool and died trying to save him.

Touched by the devotion of the people of his village,
Krishna expanded his body until the serpent's grip could
no longer hold him. Playfully he swirled the serpent
until the snake was exhausted. Then on lotus feet,
Krishna danced on the serpent's hundred heads, tram-
pling him into submission. In this dance of destruction
and devotion, Krishna churned the polluted pool into an
ocean of ambrosia. When the sweet liquid of love was
touched to the lips of the poisoned cows and cowherds,
their happy life was restored. This miraculous transformation came out of awareness of the cowherds' devotion
to Krishna and from his love for them.

Whenever he could, Krishna helped his beloved cowherds. When they were making offerings to Indra to
stop the fury of the rain clouds, he intervened once
again. Indra had commanded thunder, lightning, and
torrents of rain to destroy the cows and the cowherds.
Playfully Krishna held up in one hand a magic mountain as an umbrella to protect the endangered Gopas
and their cattle. All were delighted by the love that
sheltered them. At first amazed that the simple son of a
cowherd could offer so much wonderful care, eventually the Gopas became aware of his devotion as divine
affection that infected all of them. To fulfill his commitment to the cowherds, again and again it was necessary
for Krishna to be playful. During a drought, he played

tricks on Indra himself, seducing him into providing the rain necessary to feed the cattle.

I, too, have had to learn that if I am to live out the love I feel for those under the umbrella of my own devotion, I must accept the necessity of committing myself again and again. A short time after my dream of my father's other son, I dreamed about my grandson. Like the baby Krishna, Daren brought his playful mischief to instruct me in devotion to the ongoing endlessness of my endeavors to help those I love.

The dream began with my diapering Daren to ready him for a wonderful trip we would make together. Soon we sat side by side, heading off together in my car to share some exciting adventure. Pleased with myself for having taken care of all the baby's needs, triumphantly I turned to smile at him.

Diapered and delighted in his car seat, in expression of our usual wordless communication, Daren returned my smile. Almost immediately I recognized that he had met my own expression with a subtler one—his own wry grin. At the same time, in a gesture precocious for his age, he motioned over his left shoulder with his extended right thumb pointing toward something I had overlooked.

Turning my gaze to follow the guidance of his pointed gesture, to my astonishment I became aware that he was turning my attention to the back seat of the car. There sat a twin of my grandchild, differing from Daren only in that this child had a full load in his pants. Again I was to understand a new necessity that required my rededication to diapering.

In this segment of the broken circle of the life I live, the infant aspect of my newborn god Krishna manifests himself both as my grandson, Daren, and as my daily devotion to him and all the everyday others I love. In his later development into an erotic young man in erotic dalliance with the Gopis, Krishna serves to direct my own emotionally playful courtship of the three "daughters" my sons have herded home into the fold of our family.

As a young man, Krishna became the group lover of the Gopis. Playful dalliance with the Gopi women cowherds demonstrates yet another aspect of that god's immersion in personal relationship and of the bliss of his loving devotion. These courtships are characterized by irresistible charm, enchantment, and his antic overcoming of social distance through mischievous mockery of personal restraint. The entrancingly seductive invitation of the music of Krishna's flute flouts moralistic margins and breaks the boundaries of convention. Krishna captivates the hearts and excites the desires of all who hear his boisterous call to a carnival of rollicking play. Delightfully intoxicating and enchanting, the irresistible invitation of his flute distracts the hearer's heart away from attention to routine activity, enchanting her to revel instead in an instant of ecstasy.

Krishna's engagement with the Gopis began mischievously on one of those last days of the month when the cowherd women regularly bathe in the river, leaving their lovely clothes on the bank. Running merrily into the water to wash themselves, soon the women were so absorbed in this activity that they ignored what was happening on the riverbank. Krishna came quietly, and playfully he picked up their clothes. Piling the colorful clothes on his shoulder, he carried the garments to a place of hiding. Then taking a handful of the most colorful clothes, he climbed to the top of a tree at the river's edge. From the treetop he called to the cowherd women, teasingly telling them that not even their goddess had been able to protect their clothes from his capture.

Upset at their unexpected losses, the women pleaded for the return of their clothing. Laughing aloud, Krishna backed away from the riverbank, telling the Gopis that if they wanted their clothes returned, each would have to come to him on her own. In desperation, covering the embarrassment of her nakedness with her hands, one by one each Gopi approached Krishna, alternately begging and demanding the return of her clothing.

Each Gopi came to Krishna with her hands held in a manner she hoped would hide her breasts and the meeting of her thighs. But nearing him, each naked maiden was told that he would not return her clothes unless she clasped her hands over her head. Seeming to insist on this exposure only so he could get a full erotic view of her body, Krishna got each Gopi to reveal the nakedness of her personal self to his loving look. As she presented herself with hands held high, unwittingly each assumed a ritualized attitude of reverent devotion to the gods. Smiling with satisfaction at each woman's surrender, quickly compelled by compassion, Krishna returned the clothes to any woman who willingly approached him.

Krishna's seeming seduction of each cowherd woman ends with his having her reveal herself, experience the pleasure of personal contact, and reverentially reclaim what is hers. From then on the Gopis experienced the ecstasy of being as emotionally engaged to Krishna as he was to each of them.

This personalized devotion was dramatically demonstrated in their erotic circle dance. Whenever the Gopis heard the mischievously melodic sound of Krishna's flute, each was invited individually according to her own character. A shy one sang along softly to the sound of his soft song. A passionate one followed frenetically the erotically arousing rhythms she alone had heard. A solitary Gopi sat at home silently listening to the inner mood music his flute implanted within her imagination.

Moved to follow the flute's invitation into the forest, each cowherd woman met a figure of Krishna meant for her alone. As each danced with her own Krishna, she found his kindness and concern specially suited to her own nature. Multiplying himself into the perfect partner of each, Krishna drew the individual Gopis into a circle of sisterhood in which they could dance happily free of competition or jealousy. In accepting his embrace, each found herself fulfilled, lost in love that invited no envy from the others.

This is the Yoga known as Bhakti, the Hindu spiritual release offered by open expression of emotion overflowing from a full heart. It frees us from the apprehensive assumption that there is only so much love to go around, and from the fear that if one gets more it means another will receive less. In the circle dance, Krishna becomes the beloved of each. None need be neglected.

In his discourse on love, Krishna was approached by one of the Gopis who hoped he would set her heart at ease. Poignantly she pleaded:

> In this world, there are different types of love and different types of lovers. Some people are capable only of returning the love given to them. There are others who behave in the opposite way. They give love without expecting love in return. Even if they are not loved, they love others since it is their nature to do so. There is a third category of

people who, even when they are loved, do not
return the affection shown to them; nor are they
affected if they are not loved by others. Krishna,
please tell us which of these types is the best and
why.[3]

Smiling softly, Krishna took seriously both the wonder and the worry in her inquiry. He told her that those
who love with the expectation of receiving love in return are selfishly seeking their own comfort and happiness. People pair in this way to use one another rather
than for the sake of simply loving and being loved. He
went on to explain that the second type, those who love
though there is no love given in return, offer affection
like that of parents for their children. They are kind and
compassionate caretakers who can be depended on to be
good friends.

The third type includes people incapable of returning
the love offered to them. As examples he cited the
self-contained, detached worshipers of Shiva who neither need love for themselves nor enjoy their affection
for others. They are so self-satisfied that their hearts
hunger for nothing more. Having no need of the love of
others, they are distant and indifferent. Ungratefully, at
times they may accept others' appreciation without responding in return. At worst, by contemptuously pa-
tronizing the giver of love, they are capable of betraying
anyone who cares about them.

Krishna went on to offer his own alternative. He
pointed out that he himself did not always accept the
love showered upon him by the Gopis. Sometimes for a
moment he held back on returning it as a way of inviting his devotees to love him even more. But the fulcrum
of the fullness of Krishna's love lay in his willingness to

devote himself entirely to each of them, just as he invited each to envelop herself in dedication to him.

Either can experience the other at one time as an infant and at another as an adult. Each assumes the attitude of mother to the child aspect of the other, as well as that of the child to his or her mothering. Alternately, each may be experienced as the mouth of the crying, hungry infant or as the offered breast of the great mother nursing the needs of the other's infant longing. "So it is," Krishna assured the Gopi, "I am your life, and you are mine."

In becoming conscious of Krishna, this attitude of easy interplay has come to me by way of the Gopi daughters who are the women my sons have chosen. Prior to their entry into my family life, my middle-aged nightdreams already included encounters with younger women, but each appeared as an object existing only to augment my own personal pleasure.

The gathering of my Gopis has broken the circle of my earlier otherwise predictably self-centered night voyages. More and more often now I dream of being surrounded by little girls whose attention I engage by sleight-of-hand tricks and whom I entertain by making music to which they are delighted to dance. Occasionally, older women out of my own childhood also appear in my dreams. But they have become sweeter, more loving mothers than I can remember ever having had.

NOTES

1. Kamala Subramanian, *Srimad Bhagavatam* (a condensation of the *Bhagavata Purana*) (Bombay: Bharatiya Vidya Bhavan, 1981).

2. In one version these creatures were originally the six ascetic sons of the grandfather who had ended up in the underworld because of their unwillingness to populate the earth.

3. Subramanian, op. cit., p. 398.

Chapter 9

Therapeutic Devotion

When we willingly ignore the expectations of others and the constraints of convention, we can get away with almost anything. For years I had honored Shiva in both my personal and my professional life by assuming a shamelessly disruptive posture. The same outrageous behavior worked wonders as a psychotherapist. I got to choose the patients with whom I would work. It was not so much that the disorderly conduct of therapy brought me honor and fame as that it afforded notoriety. Paralleling the image of personal eccentricity that made it possible for me to misbehave as much as I pleased in my personal life, maverick management of my career operated equally well in allowing me to work as I wished. The reputation for power is power. I was richly rewarded with many more patient referrals than I had time to take on.

At first I tried setting up a waiting list. That was a mistake. During the delay, the person waiting for a consultation came to expect so much that our long-anticipated appointment was doomed to disappointment. Additionally, even though the patient might turn out to be someone I knew I could help, there was no guarantee that I would choose to do so. It was unfair to both of us to wait weeks for an appointment that might easily end up as no more than a one-shot screening during which one or the other of us might decide not to go on with the work.

I wanted to feel free to choose whether I would be willing to work with any particular person. By not charging for any initial consultation in which either of us chose not to go on, I relieved myself of any obligation of spending extended hours of my life each week with anyone whose company provided me no pleasure. I would not willingly curtail this arbitrary ease with any unnecessary obligation accrued by the new patient's having had to endure a long wait before we met.

Instead, when a workhour opened up, I simply invited the next person who called me to come on in and see if we liked each other well enough to work together. When my writing first came to the attention of the audience I had in mind, this self-selection process worked very well. My books have never been advertised or reviewed in any newspaper or periodical of consequence. Made popular only by word of mouth, I gradually gained a reputation as an underground cult figure. As a result, prospective patients who came to see me were often exactly the sort of people I sought. Unfortunately, as my writings became more generally popular, they became less satisfactorily self-selective. Readers responding to what they perceived as a pop psychology process of simple self-improvement began to seek my help. They were not at all what I had in mind. Soon it became clear that often I would have to meet with four or five or more of these people before I found one with whom I wished to work.

At the time of our first meeting, prospective patients seeking psychotherapy are suffering hard times. I, on the other hand, either may be enduring difficulty or enjoying an era of easy living. But at the moment of our meeting, even if I am in one of the softer segments of the broken circle, I try to remember how much of my life has already been hard and how much more hard time may yet lie ahead. I will not willingly add yet another needlessly unhappy experience to the uninvited agonies already imposed by external necessity. The hours I spend with my patients constitute an important part of how I live this time of my life.

My conviction that I can contribute to the prospective patient's expanded options for personal happiness is a condition necessary but not sufficient for my making a commitment. Earlier I had also insisted that I experience promise of the patient eventually becoming personally meaningful to me. In trying to predict this outcome, I must have made errors of underestimating how much some of those I did *not* choose might have come to mean to me had I taken the time to get to know them better.

Additionally, some relationships that seemed to show early promise did not work out well. I now regret how I treated some of those people. Early in my career, I dealt with initial overestimations by unwittingly offering carelessly poor work that led the patient to leave without our having become aware of my initial error. Later I learned to confront the patient with brutally cold detachment, saying with simple Shiva savagery that our relationship had been a mistake, and so we would stop.

More recently I have tried to maintain the devotion of my commitment by taking full responsibility for my error. This kinder Krishna consciousness requires my privately understanding and rectifying (as well as I am able) the personal flaws in myself that have been obscured by my finding fault with the patient. I am no longer willing to punish a patient for an emotional problem that is mine alone.

Along with that shift in my therapeutic posture, the second condition (founded on future promise for a personally meaningful relationship) for my willingness to work with a prospective patient is now grounded in my finding the person satisfactory *as is* at our first meeting. No matter how unaccepting the patient may be of who he or she is, my choosing to commit myself to our work together depends on my enjoying being with the patient from the outset. It does not depend on any of the improvements anticipated by the patient. I am willing to end up wherever our work together might lead. I start out already unconditionally accepting the patient's present personality without attachment to any presumed future promise of our relationship. Otherwise I am unable to avoid meddling in the patient's management of his or her life in ways that incur unnecessary impasses in my attempts to manage my part of the therapeutic process.

The therapeutic impasse is a needless power struggle between the patient and the therapist. Most often it begins with the therapist trying to pressure the patient toward something he or she is not ready to do. Lessening the likelihood of such struggles requires my choosing patients with whom, from our first meeting, it pleases me to spend my time. More frequent in my earlier therapeutic disruptions, these unfortunate impasses now occur only when demanded by therapeutic necessity. My more devotional mode makes it easier for me to endure their temporary distress long enough to circle back into the easier aspects of my relationship with a patient. Overall, in this time of increased Krishna consciousness, I see fewer patients and meet with them more often. Curiously, now that I am clearer that it is up to them to decide how much is enough, my more recent patients tend to stay in therapy longer than those whose lives I had earlier imagined myself managing.

I am no longer willing to treat patients who seem too difficult. In no case will I take on a patient I believe I cannot help. There is already enough in my life about which I can do nothing. Voluntarily committing myself to situations in which inevitably I will be helpless and despairing is foolhardy and irresponsible.

When I do not have time, I ask if the caller wants another name. Some insist I'm the only therapist they want to see. Some have heard things about me that make them determined to see me in particular. Others are simply stubbornly set to get their own way. How long would they have to wait before I have free time? they may ask. My answer is always the same. I say that I do not know when I will have free time. It might be soon or it might be a long way off. I do not keep a waiting list.

During the first hour I attempt to create an atmosphere of acceptance of what the patient chooses to present. My posture and attitude are meant to communicate my interest in getting to know the patient, as well as my willingness to let the patient get to know me. I do not take a history, preferring instead to allow circumstances of the patient's life to evolve in a natural sequence. This unfolding will be determined by the *patient's* needs and experiences rather than by any preconceived notions of my own about personal development or clinical pathology.

I am attempting to get to know who this person is, what hurts, and what resources are available for dealing with stress and pain. If it does not seem intrusive, I share small bits of my own experience to let the patient begin to know who I am.

The clarity and directness of my responses show the

patient that I know what I am doing. By allowing the story to unfold in the patient's own way and at his or her own pace, I attempt to communicate that I believe that the patient knows best how to provide the other half of the dialogue.

The safe, nurturant ambience that evolves is one in which nothing said will be met with criticism, punitive confrontation, or a tone that indicates that the patient is doing anything but exactly what it is he or she must do at that time. If we are well met, the patient will come away with a sense of having done it all just right and an understanding that I am completely satisfied that we have each done just what we needed to do with each other.

The patient's need for therapy coupled with my confidence that I could be of help are necessary but not in themselves sufficient conditions to my choosing to do the work. In choosing to spend some hours of my time with this person, I have already asserted that I am satisfied with the patient just as he or she is. Should the patient want to alter the way he or she lives, I am committed to offering expert services to promote awareness of what is wanted and of any self-defeating patterns that prevent fulfillment of those desires.

But the patient is already acceptable to me. I don't need the patient to change. I may grow to care for this person, but I do *not* care how he or she lives. I will do the job of heightening awareness about self and how that life is lived. What the patient does with this increased consciousness is not my concern. My wish is to make myself known to the patient, to get to know the other person, and to enjoy the rewards of knowing that I am working as well as I can. "Progress" in therapy is the patient's affair. If therapy is an educational experience for the patient, it is one in which I begin the work by accepting him or her as a student who attains an "A" for the course on the first day of class. After that, it is up to the patient what he or she gets out of the experience.

I have radically changed my therapeutic approach from the disruptively cutting swath of Kali's terrible sharp sword to the devotionally sublime call of Krishna's soft, sweet flute. My work has been transformed from a pseudosurgical intervention into a quasicourtship dance. Metaphorically, this shift sounds so seductive that it is necessary to sort out any implication of explicit sexual aspects the reader might otherwise infer.[1]

The sexual longings that arise between patient and therapist may be viewed as expressions of transference and countertransference. If so, they require careful therapeutic analysis. Instead, these desires may be understood as predictable, natural erotic responses of two people who like each other and have the opportunity to spend extended time alone together. Viewed from that perspective, the matter requires no further analysis.

In either case, the acting out of explicit sexuality between patient and therapist is always countertherapeutic. It parallels the confusing double roles of an incestuous family. In a therapeutic relationship, sex might be good fun, but it is always bad politics.

Albert Ellis is one of the therapists who view most sexual longings between patient and therapist as the normal biosocial desires that would occur "if the same participants encountered each other for any length of time in a non-therapy relationship . . ."[2]

Even so, he sees great disadvantages in a male therapist having intercourse with a female patient.

[He] may well prove to be a disappointing sex-love partner to her. He will probably end the affair within a fairly short period of time—especially if he is having sex relations with several of his other patients, too! He is likely to be sexually rather than amatively attracted to his patient, while she is likely to be much more emotionally involved with him. He may well be consciously or unconsciously exploiting her sexually. He will often encourage her to be dishonest with him, as a patient, because she is interested in continuing with their sex-love relationship. He may be sorely tempted to gratify her sick needs for being loved, and make her unusually dependent on him rather than help her to become truly independent in her own right. He will tend to leave her without a suitable therapist if their sex affair ends. He will lose objectivity in diagnosing and treating her. . . .

Legally he may be convicted of statutory rape, especially if he induces the patient to have sex relations with him in order to help her treatment. Professionally, he is engaging in unethical behavior and may well be dismissed from the reputable societies of which he is a member. He also gets in difficulties with his other patients, particularly with jealous females with whom he is not having any sex relations! . . . He may easily be blackmailed . . . and he may well draw down upon himself the wrath of a large segment of his community.[3]

There is more to the problem of dealing with sexuality in the therapy relationship than just these practical, rational considerations. For all of us, sex can be a ready arena in which a variety of willful struggles may be enacted. In any relationship, sexuality may serve other needs, such as dependency, power, or even hostility. The psychotherapeutic alliance is especially vulnerable to such distortions. In any case, the therapeutic goal of self-awareness demands that no transaction go unexamined.

Some years ago, the psychoanalytic mode predominated. In that era, the young male therapist was often tempted to try to talk the patient out of her threateningly tempting sexual longings. By reducing these feelings to nothing more than "positive transference," he would attempt to interpret them away. This turned out to be an uneven contest.

> . . . the hysteric makes sexuality out of the therapist's science, or the therapist makes science out of the sexuality. In this affair, the hysteric has the advantage, there being more sex to science than vice versa.[4]

During the sixties and seventies, humanistic psychotherapy began to come to the fore. In its emphasis on feeling, on experiencing things in the here and now, and on the therapeutic alliance as a beautiful encounter between two struggling human beings, the same problems continue to arise, but now they are understood by the therapist in a new way.

A young, attractive female patient may still tell her middle-aged male therapist that she is in love with him. Letting him know how wonderful he is, she will make it clear that she would like to go to bed with him. Too often the humanistic therapist can see her point.

He experiences her as truly appreciating how "together" he is. He forgets how often in analysts' offices beautiful twenty-year-old women have fallen madly in love with dull, bald, paunchy, sixty-year-old men. The phenomenon is called transference. Any man sitting in his therapist's chair would have seemed as engaging to a patient caught up in the flow of the therapeutic process.

The impasse that occurs in that process is not caused by the patient's sexuality but by the therapist's attachment to it. Ethically bound not to have sex with the patient, he may still hedge about giving up his attachment to that wish. This can lead to his seeking the fantasy satisfaction that goes with a nonexplicit sexual game.

Though he chooses not to have sex with the patient, he still wants to experience the patient's attraction to him as though it were a personal response to his charm. He is careful not to "reject" the patient's "love," lest he hurt her feelings. It has been noted that "because feeling has been so blown up recently people have come to take it as the panacea for therapy."[5]

The outcome of such attachment games was clearly demonstrated in one supervisory seminar session. A therapist and his female patient had come to talk about their problems of her continuing insistence that they make love. He contended that he had told her very clearly that they would not. It turned out that he had also let her know that he was sure that under other circumstances, their making love would have been a beautiful experience.

Ostensibly his only reason for refusing was that it would not be good for her. Professional responsibilities did not permit him such an untherapeutic indulgence. Despite his making all of this clear to her, he complained, she went on trying to convince him that he should change his mind.

I asked the patient what message she had been getting from her therapist. Her response was clear and perceptive: "When he says 'no' that way, I hear him telling me, 'not yet, we're still negotiating.' " The patient recognized that the therapist's attachment to his sexual longings was far more significant than all his talk about professional responsibility.

Much of this struggle might have been avoided. From the beginning, the patient's sexual overture could have been bracketed into the therapeutic process. In the absence of attachment, the therapist's concentration on the work could have transformed the overture into further grist for the therapeutic mill. The appropriate therapeutic response would have communicated this message: "Your sexual fantasy about our relationship will give you the opportunity to learn more about yourself."

Most therapists understand at the outset that sexual attachment to patients is countertherapeutic. Still, like young Augustine, they entreat: "Lord, grant me chastity and continency . . . but not yet."

Free of attachment, the therapist might have realized that, after all, it was only sex. This would have allowed his getting on with enough understanding to interpret the meaning of the sexual material in terms of the context in which it arose and of the associations that accompanied it. In this way, the exchange could have turned out to be yet another way for the patient to become more aware of the underlying meaning of her behavior.

It is degrading for a woman to offer sex to a man she hires as a therapist and to whom she already pays many dollars an hour. Often it turns out that the patient feels she does not have enough to offer as a person, or that she has hidden needs to control the therapist, to rob him of his power, to prove that she cannot depend on him, etc. Sacrificing awareness of these unconscious motives can be very costly.

Even when the therapist appears to shift into an exclusively therapeutic interest in the patient's sexuality, another teasing impasse may ensue. "In the interests of the treatment," he may pressure the patient to turn him on with graphically detailed descriptions of her fantasies.

It is possible to avoid this potential impasse without loss to the patient. The therapist can suggest: "You have begun to show how costly it is for you to miss knowing any part of yourself. It will be easier for you to let yourself experience these sexual fantasies if you remember that there is no need for you to report them to me. As with anything that comes to mind, you may talk of them if you wish, and I will listen as I always do. I have no need to know everything that you think or feel."

Later on in the therapeutic relationship, the patient and the therapist may develop simpler, more direct sexual feelings for one another. People who spend time together in an intimate setting often develop sexual as well as other feelings of mutual attraction. Such feelings may be largely free of transference and countertransference implications. If the therapist is concentrating on promoting the therapeutic process, there will be no attachment great enough to distract from doing the work. The therapist who is not aware of the dangers and who accepts such sexual longings will be especially vulnerable to enmeshing himself in erotic impasses.

The therapeutic impasse can arise as easily out of negative attachment to the pain of hostility as out of the positive attachment to the pleasure of sex. Feeling that I cannot possibly bear a painful experience is as binding as insistence that I simply cannot do without a pleasurable one. Concentration on the work allows the therapist liberation from both kinds of impasses.

In the devotional relationship, trust is essential to the founding of the therapeutic alliance. How am I to communicate to the patient I am an attentive, understanding listener ready to respect the feelings and beliefs expressed? Assuring encounter requires my sensitively accurate reflection of the patient's feelings.

NOTES

1. Sheldon Kopp, *Back to One: A Practical Guide for Psychotherapists* (Palo Alto, Calif.: Science and Behavior Books, 1977), pp. 108–12. An earlier version of the materials on sex in psychotherapy appeared originally in this earlier work.

2. Albert Ellis, "To Thine Own Therapeutic Lust Be True???: A Rational-Emotive Approach to Erotic Feelings in the Psychotherapy Relationship," a paper read at the symposium "Erotic Feelings in the Psychotherapy Relationship—Origins, Influence, and Resolutions, American Psychological Association convention, Philadelphia (August 31, 1963), p. 3.

3. Ibid., pp. 6–7.

4. Leslie H. Farber, *The Ways of the Will: Essays Toward a Psychology and Psychopathology of Will* (New York: Basic Books, 1966), p. 109.

5. James Hillman, "The Feeling Function" in *Jung's Typology*, by Marie-Louise von Franz and James Hillman (New York: Spring Publications, 1971), p. 82.

Chapter 10

Worthy of Trust

Trust cannot be established simply by saying: "I hear you. I understand. I care." It is not what I say but what I do that allows the patient's experiencing the safe, nurturant atmosphere within which the therapeutic process can thrive. This depends totally on how lovingly I treat the patient.

If we are to establish a trusting work alliance, the patient must be offered an easy experience of being clearly heard and understood. Paradoxically, the earliest meetings during which I attempt to establish this trust occur at a time when I hardly know the patient. I need to communicate some sense of empathy when my understanding of the patient is just beginning to evolve.

Busy formulating hypotheses in my head about the nature of the patient's problems, I may be tempted to show I understand by offering interpretations of the underlying meaning of the patient's behavior. This is a mistake. Even if some of my interpretations are correct, they are likely to be premature. If a patient is not ready to receive the awareness that might later be made available by a well-timed interpretation, the too-early impact is more likely to be one of feeling assaulted than understood. Depth interpretations are to be avoided during the first phase of therapy.

The kind of understanding that encourages trust during this phase can be attained through use of the therapeutic intervention called reflection of feelings. I listen carefully to what is being described about the patient's life situation, sense of self, or experience of being in therapy. Attempting to put myself in the patient's place, I then formulate what seems to be the central feeling that the patient is expressing. This feeling, aimed at offering heightened awareness of what is already emotionally experienced, I reflect back to the patient.

This intervention of reflecting feelings was developed by Carl Rogers many years ago as the central technique of his then revolutionary client-centered psychotherapy.[1] Early in his work, Rogers grew dissatisfied with having the counselor's role defined as distant and superior, as the expert authority who handed down interpretations. He saw the client and the therapist as equals and so felt that the therapist's attitude should be respectful, open, and permissive. The therapist's orientation was to be phenomenologically focused on the world as the client experiences it rather than on objective "reality" (compared with what?) or on a search for "hidden" unconscious dynamics. Rogers felt that any diagnostic assumptions about the client would be presumptuous and detrimental. Instead, the nondirective therapist treats the patient with "unconditional positive regard" and respect for the client's feelings. The client gets a sense of being understood by being helped to experience his or her own feelings more clearly by the therapist's nonjudgmental reflection of what the client has said. In such an atmosphere, Rogers believes the client will solve his or her own problems.

The term "reflection" turned out to be an unfortunate

label for this intervention. Young therapists have sometimes taken it to mean that what is required is a simple
two-dimensional mirroring of what the patient is saying.
An apocryphal "dialogue" makes this point painfully
clear:

PATIENT: "Doctor, I'm having lots of trouble."
THERAPIST: "You feel that you are having lots of
trouble."
PATIENT: "My life is rotten. I'm a miserable failure."
THERAPIST: "You feel that your life is rotten and that
you're a miserable failure."
PATIENT: "It just doesn't seem like there's anything
worth living for."
THERAPIST: "You feel that there's nothing worth liv-
ing for."
PATIENT: [The patient gets up out of his chair and
goes to the open window of the therapist's office.
The patient jumps out of the window, screaming as
he falls.] "Ahhhh . . ."
THERAPIST: "Ahhhh . . ."

The problem here is twofold. The therapist in this
vignette does nothing more than echo the patient's words.
There is no appreciation of what it must be like to
suffer the patient's situation, and no empathy is communicated. There is evidence of careful listening to the
patient's words but failure to show any emotional impact of the patient's experience. As the therapist, I must
try to put myself in the patient's place. I need not feel
sympathy for the patient's attitude to be able to identify
with it.

Appreciation is required not only of the patient's
words but also of who speaks these words. I try to sense
what it feels like to be the patient and what it must feel

like to be telling all this to a stranger. To communicate my empathy I must offer a certain freshness to the feedback. I attempt to summarize in new words the central feeling behind the patient's statements. Only this will allow the patient to experience really having been heard. This freshness may even deepen the patient's own understanding of what is being felt.

By way of example, I will reframe the earlier apocryphal dialogue:

PATIENT: "Doctor, I'm having lots of trouble."

THERAPIST: "You want me to understand that this is a very tough time for you."

PATIENT: "My life is rotten. I'm a miserable failure."

THERAPIST: "Everything is so awful that you feel your life is ruined and that you can't do anything to make it any better."

PATIENT [Cries silently, brushing the tears away.]

THERAPIST: "The tears come, but you brush them away as if you had no right to cry about how unhappy you feel."

PATIENT: [Cynically constraining his crying] "What's the use of crying?"

THERAPIST: "You feel so hopeless that part of you tries bitterly to avoid any more disappointment. But inside, another part of you goes on weeping, hoping that somehow the pain will end."

PATIENT: [Sobbing more openly, the patient mutters] "Sometimes I just want to end it all."

THERAPIST: "You hurt so bad that sometimes you feel like killing yourself rather than go on suffering unbearable pain in a life you feel helpless to change."

PATIENT: [Now unrestrained tears are accompanied by soulful sobbing and moans of anguish. This continues uninterrupted by the therapist. After several minutes, seeming somewhat relieved, the patient goes on to describe to the therapist the troubles in his life.]

At the beginning of therapy, reflection of feelings is the intervention called for whenever the patient has completed reporting some segment of description of a life situation, an inner state, or of the relationship with the therapist. This will result in a deepening of the patient's experience of his own feelings, a continuing flow of fresh material, and a gradual building of trust in the therapeutic alliance.

However, it will soon become evident that sometimes the reflections are absorbed by the patient without apparent impact. The very manner in which the patient attempts to respond to the intervention prevents broader or deeper exploration of what is going on inside.

The patient may go on to introduce additional content, but all of it will be presented in a characteristic style that by its very nature serves to limit any further self-awareness. This impasse constitutes the emergence of neurotic character style. The called-for intervention is confrontation. The work at this point requires that I shift my concentration from content to form, focusing away from *what* is being said to *how* it is being said.

In his seminal work on character analysis, Wilhelm Relich points out, ". . . the patient must first find out that he defends himself, then by what means, . . . [and] finally, against what."[2]

Confrontational character analysis works best when held off for the first few sessions to give the patient's full style a chance to surface. The patient will be consciously putting forward symptoms and life problems in hope of discussing, exploring, and resolving them.

In contrast, the character style will be lived out, often

without awareness. Even if partially conscious of these attitudes, the patient is unlikely to understand all the ways in which they restrict the range of his or her experience. Should there be awareness of some aspect of this style, and dissatisfaction with its effects, it is still unlikely to be viewed as a problem about which anything can be done. No matter how aware or dissatisfied a person is with this character style, it is likely to be experienced as a fact of nature. For the patient, it is just the way he or she is.

The patient's stylized approach may be an unwittingly self-limiting attitude of skepticism, intellectualization, and detachment. Or it may instead be one of compliance, passivity, and disinterest, or of denial, shallowness, and unfounded optimism. The varieties of character configurations are many.

Whatever the variations, all neurotic character styles have certain common characteristics. Such styles are protective attitudes developed early in life as necessary armor against an emotionally destructive environment. At first they served to keep the patient safe from the surrounding dangers. Additionally, they offered protection against internal anguish too overwhelming to be borne at the time.

Now in adult life these attitudes are self-maintaining. In limiting the patient's experience of anxiety, they also restrict the possibilities for new experience. Ironically, in this way they prevent realization that the original danger has passed.

As with all avoidant defenses, these attitudes have been set up to hold off catastrophe. Unexpected experiences and risky behaviors are limited. The patient does not do anything new and "dangerous." The prohibited act is avoided. The unconsciously dreaded terrible consequences do not come about. Thus every bit of avoidant behavior is reinforced by the absence of consequent catastrophe.

Dealing with the patient's neurotic style is a twofold problem for the therapist. If the necessary confrontational work of character analysis is not done first, none of the subsequent interpretative interventions will promote the therapeutic process. For example, if I make the error of neglecting this early work with an obsessional patient, we will go on into what we mistake for progress in our misalliance. Not having recognized and worked through her neurotic style, she continues intellectualizing all her experiences in a way that protects her from fear of losing control of her feelings. The result is that later interpretations simply facilitate her becoming the most insightful neurotic in the Washington metropolitan area.

A second oversimplified example could involve my negligence in this early work with an hysteric. Neglecting to confront him about his style of romantic denial of bad feelings, I participate in the mutually seductive misalliance of our both being very special creatures. Later interpretations result in seemingly miraculous transformations of the patient. These changes turn out to be as unstable as our ability to maintain the magic of our union.

A second aspect of my problem as a therapist doing this work is that character analysis cannot be forced. Necessary as it is to the promotion of the outcome of the therapy, confrontation cannot be carried out as a form of coercion. Confrontation is not challenge and must never be punitive. This unfortunately labeled intervention is no more than the therapist's inviting attention to a previously ignored pattern of the patient's behavior so that awareness of it may be increased. It is true that observed behavior is always somewhat different than unobserved behavior. Still, any basic change in style can result only from the patient's curiosity based on growing understanding of this style, of its origins, and of the costs of this protection.

At worst, confrontation can be misused by the therapist to criticize how the patient behaves and as an attempt to force change. In its most extreme form, this constitutes the basic intervention of the attack therapy of the Synanon style of self-help for drug addicts, and the barnstorming workshops of certain itinerant encounter group leaders.

Confrontations need never be punitive, blaming, or coercive. The therapeutic intervention of confrontation involves calling the patient's attention to observable aspects of behavior that have been ignored up to that point. This is done simply by offering observations without blame or criticism. It is a way of directing the patient's attention to how he or she behaves. The purpose is promotion of the process of self-discovery by increasing awareness. I make no effort to judge the behavior, nor do I insist that it be changed in any way.

These observations are offered most effectively by juxtaposing a number of pieces of behavior that go together to reflect the patient's characteristic attitudinal style. My primary focus is on how the patient behaves within the therapy sessions. Examples must be concrete and directly observable. Later, by pointing out similar behavior in reported interactions with other people, I can go on to how the patient's style is reflected in daily life.

To convey some sense of the accepting and respectful confrontational interventions required for character analytic work, I will present a condensed, somewhat idealized set of transactions between a male patient and his therapist. This interplay condenses work carried out over the course of many weeks. The actual process is fraught with therapist errors, false starts, unexpected impasses, and intervening materials from the patient that are not directly related to the character analysis.

PATIENT: I had a lot of trouble at work last week. The boss told me to inventory the stock. Then some emergency deliveries had to be made, so I went out to do them. When I got back, I was ready to get on with completing the inventory. It had to be done in a hurry. I was way behind schedule by then. But no sooner had I gotten started than the assistant boss got back from out of town. I had to take time out to help him catch up on things. By Friday I still hadn't finished the inventory. The boss was mad at me because of that. And the assistant boss told me I was so tense that I wasn't much help in getting him caught up, either.

THERAPIST: You had an awful lot of work this week. You tried your best, but it was just too much to do. You ended up feeling even worse because both of your bosses were dissatisfied with you. [Attempts to reflect patient's feelings.]

PATIENT: Well, they were right. I messed everything up because I just didn't work fast enough. I've never been able to please the people I've worked for. [Rejects reflection in favor of self-critical explanation.]

THERAPIST: Underneath your complaining about yourself, you must be very angry at the bosses for demanding that you do more than anyone could manage. [Unwarranted premature interpretation.]

PATIENT: Why should I get angry at them? I just feel guilty because I haven't done my job. [Rejects interpretation. Returns to self-blaming.]

THERAPIST: I've noticed that no matter what you're

telling me about, you always talk in an apologetic voice. Your shoulders sag and your head is lowered. You shake your head as if you are exasperated with yourself, and sometimes you roll your eyes as though you can't believe what a fuck-up you think you are. [Confrontation.]

PATIENT: I guess I do. I hadn't thought of it that way before. You're right to criticize me for that. It's a dumb way to look and to sound. It must make a lousy impression. I should know better.

THERAPIST: You hear my observations as criticism. You're telling me right now that you are to blame for being so hard on yourself, even though you weren't aware that's how you present yourself when you talk to me.

PATIENT: I guess I feel ashamed to tell you about how many ways I screw things up.

THERAPIST: You've told me several stories about times when you and your bosses weren't getting along at work and when you and your parents weren't getting along at home. [Cites concrete examples.] In every story, no matter what has gone wrong, you always tell the story apologetically, as though it's your fault. You always describe yourself as the guilty party. [Expands scope of confrontation.]

PATIENT: I guess I do that a lot. Without realizing it, I guess I'm always acting like I know it's all my fault. I wonder why I act that way.

THERAPIST: You begin to see that you put yourself down is the way you approach most conflicts. You're becoming aware that there must be something behind the way your manner pleads you guilty even before you are accused of being to blame. You don't know the underlying reason yet, but you can see it has an effect on all our talks. Even my observations about your behavior seem like criticisms to you that confirm just how bad you feel about yourself.

This confrontational structuring of the patient's beginning awareness of his character style would actually be built up over many sessions, a bit at a time. In that way the didactic tone of the therapist's last response would be avoided.

At this point the correct timing of the confrontation would be confirmed if the patient retold one of the stories in a fresh way that did not assume his own guilt in advance. If the character armoring was not too heavy, some of his underlying feelings might begin to emerge. Another likely possibility would be that new memories might come to mind. These would reveal early experiences and relationships in which this character formation originally took root.

In practice, confrontations such as this one must be made again and again. The content of *what* is being recounted must be ignored in favor of concentration on the form of *how* it is being told.

With a patient like this man, if the character work is not substantially accomplished during the first phase of the treatment, the result will be a sadomasochistic misalliance. The therapeutic experience then deteriorates into a stale, predictable sequence of confessions by the patient, with the therapist underscoring his faults and with the patient making new penitential resolutions to change. By then I would have found myself in the position of a judging, condemning therapist/parent of this unsatisfactory fuck-up of a patient/son.

This young man's penitential, self-blaming character style pervades his behavior and colors everything he experiences. Yet it is the only aspect of himself with which he is not dissatisfied. He must become aware that he has such a style before he can learn that it influences how he understands his life and what he communicates of himself to others.

Only then can he deepen his self-understanding by becoming conscious that his life-style is that of an accused man pleading guilty to a lesser charge to avoid being punished for a more serious offense. His plea-bargaining involves continual confession to the misdemeanor of conscious inadequacy to beat the felony counts of unconscious rage and pride. By copping a plea of being a fuck-up, he hides from himself and from others both his murderous rage against those in authority, and his grandiose superiority toward everyone else. His perfectionist standards require that he be able to do whatever is demanded of him. Lower standards obtain for other people unconsciously assessed as lesser beings.

The character analytic work required with any particular patient cannot be carried out effectively outside the context of the growing trust required for a sound therapeutic alliance. Trust in this alliance allows the character work to open the patient to new ways of experiencing. At that point I can introduce the third focus of the early work: the redefining of the patient's problems. This requires the intervention of structural questioning.[3]

A therapist may ask a patient many questions to clarify a communication, or merely to get more information. It may not be clear that all these questions direct the patient to regard some facts or feelings as more important than others. Seemingly simple questions lead the patient in irrelevant directions that might not otherwise be pursued. Consider the therapist's superficially innocuous attempts to obtain additional historical data such as "How old were you at the time?" or "Were you the youngest child in the family?"

Because of the unintended implicit burden that the therapist's questions may place on the patient, some therapists try to avoid questions completely. An apocryphal tale is told of a group therapist who was participating in a weekend encounter group workshop. He was enormously impressed with the forceful leadership of the man who was running the encounter group. As the weekend went on, the therapist realized that the leader's power seemed to lie in the fact that he never asked any questions of the group members.

Returning to his practice the following week, the group therapist decided to try to increase his own therapeutic effectiveness by emulating the encounter group leader's question-free approach. The first time that his therapy group met that week, he felt very excited. He began the session by describing to them his experience of the weekend, his recognition of the powerful non-questioning technique of the encounter group leader, and his intention to work in the same way. He concluded this statement to the group by saying, "From now on I am never, never again going to ask any questions of you people. How does that strike you?"

The majority of therapists finds that in most therapy sessions it is not possible to go very long without having to ask a question. The point then is to recognize the question as a valid therapeutic intervention. As such, it is to be used deliberately, only when called for, and with the express purpose of promoting the patient's self-awareness. As such, the goal is to increase the patient's understanding, not the therapist's.

Structural questioning is useful when the patient is describing life problems in neurotic terms. The patient defines the self as the problem (e.g., "I am inadequate, unworthy, unlovable, etc."). Nonexistent solutions to these created problems become the futile focus. Neurosis is not a matter of personal defects. It is largely a problem of attention.

Focused on a sense that there is something wrong with him or her, the patient has lost sight of the richness of possibilities in the ongoing process of life. The purpose of the intervention of structural questioning is a shift of attention to the fullness and complexity of a life seen only in terms of the impoverished verbal model inside the patient's head. Because of narrowed attention, conscious representation of life suffers from missing parts, unexamined presuppositions, and costly distortions.

The following examples of structural questioning will be presented in a single sequence, with each question occurring only once. In practice, these interventions are repeated along the way over more than one session. Each time a particular question is asked it redirects the patient's attention away from the surface structure of complaints about self-image toward expansion of awareness of some aspect of the underlying deep structure.

The patient in this instance is a high-school senior living at home with his parents and three younger brothers.

PATIENT: My trouble is that I feel inadequate all the time.

THERAPIST: Inadequate to do what? [Shifts attention from label to process.]

PATIENT: Well, it's not so much that I can't do things. It's really that I can't do anything without feeling that I'm not doing a good enough job.

THERAPIST: Not doing a good enough job for whom? [Shifts attention to missing references.]

PATIENT: For other people.

THERAPIST: Who is it specifically you don't do a

good enough job for? [Shifts attention from generalization to concrete experience.]

PATIENT: Well, mainly for my father. He's never satisfied with anything I do.

THERAPIST: How well would you have to do something for your father to be satisfied? [Shifts attention to unexamined possibilities.]

PATIENT: He wants me to be the best at everything I do. When I'm in competition, it doesn't matter how well I do a thing. If someone else does it better, then he's not satisfied with my performance. [He goes on to give examples of an essay contest and of a track meet.] Obviously my father doesn't love me.

THERAPIST: To whom is it obvious? [Rhetorical; shift of patient's attention to the fact that all he is describing are his own conclusions about the interactions with his father.] What you're saying is that your problem is that you feel inadequate all the time. It turns out that what you mean is that unless you win, your father's not satisfied with how well you perform in competitive situations. Because of that, you're sure he doesn't love you, and the reason you give yourself for why he doesn't is that you're an inadequate human being. [Summary redefinition of the patient's problem in terms of the underlying structure elicited by the questions.]

The therapist's careful use of structural questioning facilitates the patient's redefining of problems by discovery of their deeper structure. But this new awareness will not be lasting if mediated solely by this one intervention. The groundwork for its effectiveness requires that first the trust necessary to a therapeutic alliance be mediated by the intervention of reflection of feelings. The alliance will not by itself allow the patient the lasting expanded awareness that constitutes the therapeutic process. Within this are needed the new experiences promoted by the confrontations of the character analysis.[4]

NOTES

1. Carl Rogers, *Client-Centered Therapy* (Boston: Houghton Mifflin Company, 1951).

2. Wilhelm Reich, *Character-Analysis*, 3rd ed. (New York: Orgone Institute Press, 1949), p. 4.

3. Richard Bandler and John Grinder, *The Structure of Magic: A Book About Language and Therapy* (Palo Alto, Calif.: Science and Behavior Books, 1975).

4. Sheldon Kopp, *Back to One: A Practical Guide for Psychotherapists* (Palo Alto, Calif.: Science and Behavior Books, 1977), pp. 125–40.

Chapter 11

Intimate Interpretations

The combined effects of these early interventions often free the patient of his or her presenting complaints. Successful completion of this early work tempts patients to terminate therapy at this point if they accept relief from the original discomfort as all they can hope for. Without having become curious about the way he or she lives, or about an interest in an emotionally more intimate relationship with the therapist, the patient is unlikely to remain in treatment long enough and to go on to attain as yet unimagined prospects of personal happiness.

The first indication of completion of the beginning work may come in the patient's finding that there no longer seems to be much to talk about. Often this is expressed in terms of having solved the problems that first led to seeking treatment. The troubled times seem to have passed without interest in even easier living having emerged.

As always, at this point I am quite willing to accept the patient's wish to do as he or she pleases. But I am not willing to lend support to leaving in the absence of understanding the choice point that has been reached.

This has all the makings of a major impasse. If I

encourage continuation of treatment, the patient's approach/avoidance conflict will divide by displacement into a tug-of-war between us. The patient is likely to insist that it is up to me to be convincing that it is worthwhile to spend more time and money to discover deeper problems and to endure more pain.

I communicate that I am quite willing to help in making this decision about the patient's life. I can be counted on to aid the patient in choosing to leave or stay, as he or she wishes. I can also be counted on to promote the patient's doing so with his or her increased awareness of all this choice entails. I demonstrate that I do not care what he or she does. My concern involves only my commitment to continue to offer expert assistance in heightening consciousness.

I go on to communicate that the current misgivings about continuing to meet with me are very much like the doubts most people experience when they reach this threshold of the second stage of therapy. Making clear that I do not know whether it would be best to stay or to go, I invite further exploration of the matter.

My interventions are aimed at promoting the patient's awareness of freedom and responsibility in deciding what he or she will do. It is up to the patient to choose whether to join me in an extended exploration of experiencing easier living. Most of my patients continue in therapy, utilizing our alliance as a medium for deepening self-discovery.

Supported by our growing therapeutic bond of mutual trust, uncritical reflection of the patient's previously unappreciated feelings enhances an increasingly accepting sense of self. Greater flexibility is allowed through recognition of excessively stylized attitudes originally aimed at unconsciously obscuring uncomfortable impulses and imaginings. Increased awareness permits perspective eased enough for the patient to begin to experience amusement at the absurdity of his or her emotional armoring. More and more often we find ourselves laughing together at the obsolescence of the patient's now unnecessary anachronistic evasions of new experiences (and, at times, my own as well).

In an atmosphere of easier living, these awakenings also invite reemergence of long-ignored pain of earlier hard times. As concentration turns inward, again and again the patient arrives at thresholds of intensely upsetting understandings. Consciously or unconsciously, earlier self-protective obstructions recur. As a means of restoring the patient's concentration on inner experience and freeing the flow of communications, at such times I offer the therapeutic intervention of *interpretation*.

An interpretation is a formulation of the unconscious meaning of the patient's experiences or behavior. If the conception is correct and the timing right, an interpretation expands the patient's self-understanding by increasing consciousness of forgotten fantasies and ignored experiences.

Interpretations must be specific to the particular patient to whom they are offered. General explanations about what it is like for most people, about the relationship of anger to helplessness, about how shame affects behavior, etc., may be educational, but they do not empower the patient's personal explorations.

At a point when an interpretation is needed, if I do not yet have enough information for fuller formulation, often I will call attention to the sequence of psychological productions. For example, a patient describes a series of events and then trails off into obsessing about the meaning of life. I simply summarize what has been presented, saying, "Before you began philosophizing about life's meaning, you told me three stories of unsatisfactory meetings with women. Each time you told of going off to hang around with the guys, and you always ended up in a fight." this preinterpretive refocusing often allows unfolding of informative related material.

Another patient presents a long, complicated dream. I respond with silence. The patient tries to understand the dream, but little or nothing comes to mind. I merely invite attention to the recurring manifest motifs. In response to a particular dream I point out: "Again and again in the dream, there is a surge of power followed by a disaster and then a restful calm." Like refocusing on sequence, pointing out recurring motifs often leads to enough new information from the patient to enable me to make the needed interpretation.

A keener sense of the proper timing of interpretations develops gradually. It is not enough for the content to be correct. If the timing is not in phase with the patient's readiness to receive it, any interpretation disrupts and delays self-discovery.

Timing errors occur most often as premature interpretations. It is not my task as a therapist to say everything I know. I offer only what is most likely to be useful at any given point. Premature interpretations confuse the patient, arouse undue anxiety, and evoke resurgence of characteristic defenses against distress.

Driven to display my "wisdom," I do at times talk too much and interpret too early. If the patient accepts my forced feeding of untimely insight, its superficial foretaste only abates the eager edge of appetite for enduring emotional understanding. At best it is a fast-food substitute for a well-prepared diet, heightening awareness in a way that is neither nutritious nor lasting.

Though interpretations can be offered too early to be useful, missed interventions alter the alliance as well. At a time when a patient is ready to receive an interpretation, its absence can also disrupt the therapeutic process. The patient finds ways to let the therapist know that he or she feels misunderstood and that repairwork to the relationship is needed. Interpretations are better made late than never.

Years ago, a child instructed me about the patient's experience of the rightness of the timing of interpretations. I had been treating his mother and his father, both individually and as a couple. In some of their joint sessions, the parents had discussed distress over their ten-year-old son's school difficulties. He had been diagnosed as a "hyperactive child." With some success he was being treated with medicine and a behavior-modification program. The parents were concerned about their own emotional problems possibly contributing to the boy's difficulties.

There was no clear evidence of this. There *was* a good deal of indication that the boy's problems were organic in origin. I agreed to their bringing him to the office for an exploratory family session. He turned out to be a bright, highly verbal, somewhat physically overactive child. His medication calmed him enough to allow productive participation in our foursome discussion of the family.

By the end of the hour it was clear to me and to his mother and father that the boy was receiving a good deal of wholesome parenting. His participation had helped all of us to understand more of what family life in his home was all about.

Before ending the session, I asked the child what his experience had been. He answered, "I pretty much liked it, but you know, Shelly, you talk funny."

Intrigued by his comment, I asked what he meant. His response was directed to the many interpretations I had made during the hour. He said, "Well, it's not just that you don't examine people and give shots like a regular doctor. It's more that lots of times when you tell me about myself, it turns out to be something I already know, but I didn't know that I knew until you told me."

Even when content and timing are right, I must decide how elaborate an interpretation to make. No interpretation is complete. Each is a fragment of understanding. At a particular time in the therapy, I may understand a good bit more than the patient about his or her unconscious fantasies.

The extent of my interpretation is determined by material the patient is addressing at a time when further unfolding is interrupted. If I understand what made the patient anxious enough to distract attention from what was emerging, I can offer an interpretation correct in its content. Even so, it will not promote the patient's reimmersion in self-exploration if it is not offered in a *form* accessible to the patient.

An interpretation works best if it is brief, simple, and directly related to issues consciously attended to by the patient at the time it is offered. Stating it in specific and personal terms requires inclusion of details of the tale being told in an idiom of the patient's style of storytelling.

The spiral is an illuminating spatial metaphor for the development of self-understanding. Seeking the center of this circular space, the sequence of the partial interpretations follows a repeated progression that cyclically deepens understanding. By yielding to the flow of the interpretations, the patient surrenders to the whirlpool current in which he or she is caught. Released consciousness spins round and round past the same positions on the circumference of an ever-narrowing and deepening circle. At the bottom, the patient arrives at a vortex of the whirlpool out of which it is possible to spin free.

This vortex is the culmination of the therapeutic process. To facilitate the patient's immersion, I select a sequence of interpretations circling *from the rim to the center* and *from the surface to the depths*.[1] A more complete interpretation would include all of these levels of understanding plus a comprehensive formulation of how those issues arose in the past, how they are acted out in the present, and how they shape the patient's relationship with me.

An interpretation this complete is rare in therapy. Fortunately, I do *not* usually understand enough to make overwhelmingly comprehensive interventions. It is just as well! It would require a minilecture that does not fit my image of myself as the therapist.

Instead, as I begin to understand, interpretive fragments are offered one piece at a time. Each selection is guided by the patient's apparent readiness to receive it. Gradually the patient puts together the bits and pieces of offered insight to allow understandable access to a life that is more meaningful.

Criteria for selection of interpretations are *not* unbreakable rules. They are only guidelines. The fittingness of an interpretation for a particular patient at a particular point is a matter of exploration and discovery. Even an incorrect interpretation sometimes can prove useful by directing the patient's attention toward unconscious meanings and offering fresh ways of experiencing life. The patient can be counted on to correct inaccurate interpretive efforts.

Interpretive interventions are aimed at deepening the patient's understanding of unconscious fantasies and feelings. Even correct interpretations will have to be repeated again and again in different contexts if the patient is to have the time needed to integrate new understandings. It is a slow and gradual process.

No matter how expert my interpretations, patients change at their own pace. Up to a point, earlier attitudes about their lives have served them well. Changing currently ineffective attitudes may be worthwhile for the patient, but no matter how beneficial, disruptions always involve both the discomforting loss of old, familiar ways and the frightening risk of newer, untried experiences. I concentrate on heightening the patient's awareness by offering what one patient described as "a Berlitz course in the language of the unconscious."[2]

Again and again the basic spiraling sequence is a repeated "unfolding, regression and resistance, clarification and interpretation, further unfolding of new material, solidification of gain regression-resistance, and so on."[3]

Deeper and deeper we spin together into the spiral of symbiotic intimacy. I willingly serve as a symbolic container into which the patient is free to empty any aspect of his or her self so unacceptably alien as to require disowning. My offer to hold whatever part the patient disclaims is demonstrated by my acceptance in the absence of expressed emotional upset of any image into which I may be cast.

When I was a less seasoned psychotherapist, the patient's criticism, hatred, and rejection were hardest for me to hold. Later, idealized love and inflated adoration constituted an even bigger burden. Patients' positive projections kept me too keenly aware of how often I experienced myself as so much less worthy than I wished to be. Recently I experience as even more disarming a patient's evolving personality using me as a nonhuman object of his or her emotional environment. At times some patients experience me as a piece of furniture, a

reliably comfortable support needing neither appreciation nor even acknowledgment of its existence. During
these times, my main mission is to be usefully available
to the patient, uninterfering in his or her internal evolve-
ment, and undemanding of any intrusive appeal for
personal confirmation.

This dehumanization is the ultimate challenge to
Krishna-consciousness. Being treated like an inanimate
object makes me painfully aware of how uncertain I am
of my own independent identity as a self sufficiently
worthwhile to be fit for human company. This vulnerability calls for my fullest consciousness of Krishna. Completely unconfirmed by my patient, I surrender my
own emotional needs to the service of the patient. My
continuing devotion allows the patient to accept an invitation to personal interplay between us at some more
fortuitous future time. The invitation reads: "RSVP
only when it seems safe enough for you to enter into
easy living with me, at a time of your own readiness to
respond to my personal presence as I do to yours. I
offer this invitation with patient acceptance of rendez-
vous delayed until you are ready to respond."

From the outset, the patients I choose to work with
are those I experience as already offering me an experience of easy living. From the beginning I anticipate that
we are certain to find some of our future encounters
painfully troubled. It is not that I expect to avoid troubled times that will make us both feel helplessly and
hopelessly stuck. Rather it is that my dedication to that
particular person makes enduring the difficulties seem
worthwhile. Therapeutic devotion requires dedicated
commitment to sticking with the relationship through
hard times after an earlier experience of easy living.

Expression of my devotion begins with willingness to
allow myself to experience our troubles with an atten-

tive emphasis on empathy. As often as I am able, I must try to imagine how our impasses are experienced by the patient. This requires my commitment to remaining silent much of the time we spend together. I listen attentively, following the patient's lead as the relevant guide to where we are headed. If I am to understand our encounter from the patient's point of view, much of the time I must accept my own uncertainty as to what is going on. Tolerating discomfort, I must begin by bracketing out irrelevant personal concerns of my own. Only then can the distress I experience be examined as an indicator that enhances understanding of some disowned aspect of the patient's experience.

Giving priority to this focus on the patient's experience of our interplay has transformed the thrust of my interpretations of patient productions. Less and less I listen as a way of unearthing early family causes of the patient's character configuration. Shifting from Shiva to Krishna as the guiding god of my work has turned my attention full circle. The patient tells me about what has happened in the past or what is currently going on in his or her life outside therapy. Increasingly I understand these accounts as metaphoric messages about how the patient experiences some hidden aspect of the self, or as an image of how I am experienced, and of our evolving therapeutic relationship.

Consciousness of the Krishna commitment "I am your life and you are mine" involves increasingly ignoring aspects of the patient's life outside the therapy except as indirect indication of what is happening between us. Whatever the manifest content of the patient's communications, I understand our coming together as the meeting of two minds and hearts and as the alternating impact of one imagination on another. Surrendering to that symbiotic merger has allowed me to experience myself as defined by the patient's picture of me and by the unacceptable aspects of the patient's self I experience as implanted within me.

In large part, perception and understanding are determined by unconscious images that imagination imposes on every experience. Whether or not I am aware of it, I respond to the influence of the underlying structure of the patient's subjective reality. Being with a patient on a continuing basis immerses me in a psychological situation that partially transforms me to fit the structure of his or her personality system. As in all such psychological structures, neurosis operates in a self-regulating way to preserve its wholeness intact.

The patient in turn is subjected to the impact of the underlying structure of a comparable therapeutic sociopsychological system as he or she enters a context constituted by the created environment of my offering to be the therapist. *Neither of us can enter the other's situation without becoming part of it.*

The patient arrives at my office, tragic scenario in hand, but it is not a matter of simply mistaking me for someone out of the past, or recasting me as a parent of early childhood (as implied by the Freudian psychoanalytic concept of transference). Rather I enter into the patient's drama (just as he or she enters into mine). For a time we each act out whatever part the other directs us to take.

Neither of us is to blame. That's the way it has to be for a while. Gradually I become aware of the ways in which I am caught up in the patient's system. We join together in the excitement of discovery, only gradually becoming aware of the underlying structure in which we are embedded. If we manage to merge in this way, our mutually expanding consciousness shifts the scene. Shared awareness allows the therapeutic system to subsume its neurotic counterpart, increasing the impact of the therapeutic alliance as a context for the patient's personal situation. Time together gradually transforms the structure of the patient's script. As a result, ability to improvise increases, enlarging the repertoire of life-style.

If eventual therapeutic transformation of the patient is to come about, for a time I must first be willing to risk being transformed by the patient. I come to the situation with incompletely resolved complexes and residuals of my own childhood miscastings. These alone would tempt me to act out a series of inappropriate roles with the patient.

Because of this projected countertransference reaction I will at times miscast the patient into some role out of one of my own childhood scenarios. It is also certain that I will become engulfed in his or her transforming system. I am certain to be affected by both conscious and unconscious expectations of the patient. My experience at these times will be more in keeping with the patient's psychological system than with my own.

Beginning work with each new patient once evoked empty resolves. In each new encounter I was determined that *this* time, with *this* person, I would be objective. This time I would *not* be manipulated. This time I would *not* participate in his or her craziness. But every time it was the same. There was no way to remain the detached expert, no way to be separated sufficiently by professionalism that I could catch his or her act without joining the new patient in a duet. I always ended up either playing the foil or becoming the patient's dancing partner.

Often I was not sufficiently perceptive to recognize the role I played. Many times my deliberately disruptive therapy hid how caught up I was in the patient's system.

One young man came to therapy complaining about a painful lack of confidence in his own judgment. He felt that his way of seeing things was rarely accepted by others, particularly by people in authority. His father, he said, had always insisted that this patient didn't really know what he was talking about. The young man was afraid that I would treat him with the same critical contempt for his point of view.

I misunderstood his expectations as a transference reaction. Pedantically, I responded with an interpretation. I told the patient that what was really going on was that he experienced the responses of people in authority *as though* they were treating him as his critical father had. Now I understand that therapeutic intervention as an error. Instead of encouraging the patient to deal directly with the hazards inherent in our developing relationship, unwittingly I invited him to join me in playing a safe intellectual game. Cast as the good patient, he complied with my request by obsessing unproductively. He simply swapped his own script for mine.

That time-wasting, risk-avoiding, stalling routine obscured another underlying obstruction that neither of us was aware of at the time. My interpretation of the patient's attitude had explained his behavior to him, unwittingly fulfilling his miscasting of my role. Like his contemptuous father, in effect I had told this patient that I understood what he was talking about and that he did not.

In recent years my work with patients has taken a different direction. I now recognize that it is impossible to entirely avoid getting caught up in the structure of the patient's miscasting system. Instead I try to surrender willingly to that experience.

Together the patient and I submit to symbiosis. Each

of us initially attempts to miscast the other into some role that fits the dramatic structure within which we define the therapeutic scene. The patient's way of seeing me is *not* a distortion. For a time, being with the patient transforms me. I may be experienced in emotionally exaggerated or symbolically caricatured ways, but the patient's "neurotic transference" perceptions of me are accurate and must be respected.[4]

With therapeutic devotion, I draw the patient into my own treatment scenario. Though I understand that I exaggerate, I focus on our time together as if it were the most important experience in the patient's life. Implicitly I offer myself and our relationship as a metaphoric medium within which the patient may recognize otherwise obscure aspects of his or her self, clarifying how well each attitude operates in everyday life and at what cost. The therapeutic alliance is a microcosmic vessel within which refined distillations of the patient's feelings, thoughts, and actions can be clearly perceived, accepted, and altered, if modification might better serve the patient's needs.

Some patients are enthralled by the extravagant importance I assign to all that occurs in our hours together. Others are offended, accusing me of making too much of our alliance, or assuming that these inflated inferences imply that underneath it all I am an "egomaniac."

Calmly and soothingly I serve as a container for any psychological segment of the self that the patient finds too unsettling or uncomfortable to claim as his or her own. In accepting any and all of the patient's accusations and idealizations without expressing emotional upset or defensiveness, I model eventual acceptance of disowned parts of the patient's personality.

Accepting either attitude, I remain silent during most

of every session, speaking only when I believe I have something useful to say. Following the patient's lead, I intervene at those times when the patient appears to need a hand in going on with telling his or her tale. My therapeutic intercessions are paced to unblock the unfolding of memories of personal past, experiences of present problems, and fears or hopes of the fantasied future. I interpret all these psychic productions as expressions of the patient's attitudes about our time together. Interpretive offerings are intended to ease the patient's self-expression. Each approximation of understanding of what is going on between us is aimed at expanding the patient's self-awareness in the interests of increasing his or her options for experiencing easier living.

Interpretive emphasis is aimed at any as yet unacceptable aspects of the patient's self and of unspeakable attitudes in our relationship. These hidden themes I discover derivatively implied in accounts of the patient's extratherapeutic encounters or the recounting of internal experiences of dreams and fantasies. For different sorts of patients, I deliberately differ in assigning emphasis onto either the self or the relationship as the central focus of each interpretation. As needed, I also alternate the interpretive priorities for any particular patient in accordance with the pacing of his or her unfolding personality process.

Considerable literary license has been exercised in the reconstruction of the following dialogue exemplifying these intimate interpretations.[5] In actual ongoing therapy experience, over time interpretations are offered again and again, with much greater intervals allotted for their integration. Interpretive statements are never so simple, accurate, or complete as they appear to be in this densely telescoped dialogue. Each interpretation begins as a fragment of partial, imperfect understanding, only later becoming included into more elaborate insights sufficiently comprehensive to allow substantial transformations.

Each fragment is only an approximation, to be discarded or refined in response to the patient's discrediting, confirmation, or revision. My criteria for rescinding or reformulation do not depend on the patient's conscious protest or agreement. Validation is ascertained only by evidence of an interpretive intervention contributing to the continuing liveliness of our time together.

In this dialogue, the first interpretation aims at awareness of obscured aspects of the patient's personality, and the second at how these attitudes are acted out in our relationship.

PATIENT: Several of my neighbors came to my house for coffee yesterday. It didn't work out very well. Half of them talked as though being a mother was the only worthwhile life a woman can live. The others were so caught up in pursuing their careers that they didn't give a damn about their kids' needs. [Describes in detail a number of the women and what each had to say.] There was so much antagonism among them, I ended up regretting that I had brought them together in my house.

THERAPIST: You feel deeply divided about the competing priorities in your life. Part of you is pulled toward taking care of other people. Another side is pushed toward ambitiously establishing something for yourself. Becoming aware of your conflict makes you so tense that it's tempting to avoid facing that you are so at odds with yourself.

PATIENT: I know what I *should* do, but I just don't have the energy. My professional work leaves me too tired to find the right day-care setup for my child, and homemaking drains away all the energy I need to expand my private practice. [The patient is a beginning psychotherapist. By mistaking the resultant depression for the cause of the delay in resolving her problem, she denies how unsettled her conflict is. After a brief silence, she goes on, as if to an unrelated topic.] You remember my telling you about that unmarried teenage mother and baby I met? Well, the better I get to know her, the more I see what a bright, wonderful girl she is. I've decided to help by teaching her the baby-care skills she needs to be able to have some time left for herself. She has more to contend with than she can handle on her own. I also gave her the names and phone numbers of community agencies she should call. I told her exactly whom to speak to and what to ask for. I suppose I really should let her learn to do this sort of thing on her own, but it's so hard for a youngster without anyone to guide her to take care of herself. If she isn't able to be aggressive enough to get what she needs, I'll step in and throw my professional weight behind her. [There is a brief troubled silence.] I hope she won't end up feeling that I'm interfering in her growing up as a way of solving some of my own problems. But what else can I do? After all, it's not as if she can do for herself what I can do, let alone all that someone like you could do for her.

THERAPIST: You hope that when I get to see how bright and wonderful you are, I will take over and teach you whatever you need to know so you can resolve your conflict between being a mother and having a career. You imagine I could take care of you by using my knowledge and reputation to get your practice going. However much you might want me to direct your life, you also feel uneasy that I might take over to serve my own needs in the way that limits your learning to fend for yourself.

PATIENT: No, that's not it at all! I'd love to get all the help you would be willing to give me. I'm sure you'd do only what's best for me. [A long silence follows this conscious denial of her worry about what would happen if her fantasy came true. Then, as if changing the subject, she brings up early childhood material in a fresh light.] Funny, I'm remembering when I was a little girl, just after my father died. I've told you before that until that time my mother hadn't paid much attention to me. I've always felt so grateful for how devoted and protective she was after that. But right now I realize how controlling she could be. Somehow I was supposed to fill the void in her life that was left by Daddy's death. [She begins to cry quietly.] It is so upsetting to realize that now I'm not sure which of us was taking care of the other. Was she the mother, or was I? It's no wonder I feel so hurt and angry at you when no matter how much I do to please you, you won't take care of me. Talking to you makes clear the price I pay when I won't run my life on my own. I hate it when I can count on you to care for me only in ways that make me more independent.

How well her words capture the spirit of Krishna's caring.

NOTES

1. Sheldon Kopp, *Back to One: A Practical Guide for Psychotherapists* (Palo Alto, Calif.: Science and Behavior Books, 1977), pp. 145–48.

2. Ibid., pp. 152–53.

3. Robert J. Langs, *The Technique of Psychoanalytic Psychotherapy, Vol. II* (New York: Jason Aronson, 1974), p. 435.

4. Sheldon Kopp, *This Side of Tragedy: Psychotherapy as Theater* (Palo Alto, Calif.: Science and Behavior Books, 1977), pp. 56–61.

5. Like all of my literary accounts of experiences with patients, this reconstructed therapeutic devotional dialogue has been fictionalized to eliminate identifying data about any particular patient. It consists instead of a distilled composite of experiences of this kind.

Chapter 12

Coping with Contradictions

Times keep changing. They just won't stand still. No one is spared repeated rounds of joy and sorrow. The soothing consistency of some experiences offers enough ease to evoke a blissful feeling of Nirvana. Too soon, the harsh necessities of samsara's demandingly painful disruptions are certain to shatter the complacency that accompanies our pleasures. After a time, easier times are available once again. Each change must be met on its own terms. Each day's experience invites its own attitude.

The many gods of the Hindu pantheon offer an array of appropriate alternatives for dealing with these cycles of constancy and change. We need not believe in the literal existence of the gods to benefit from their instructiveness as metaphors. When our attitude reflects an aspect of a god unsuitable to our situation, we take easy times for granted, suffer our troubles excessively, and miss opportunities offered by each segment of time's broken circle. We all endure times of change that can be neither explained nor controlled. If we surrender to their eternal enigma, acceptance of these changes brings comfort and congruence that help us to cope with the otherwise unsettling alternation.

Coping creatively with change requires both destructive and constructive approaches. Even when we move from bad to better times, disorienting turnarounds always accompany transitions. Ending the old can be difficult even when it involves loss of familiar troubles to enter unprepared into easier living. Transition is a time when the old god has gone and the new god has not yet arrived. Forgetting the past is a sacrifice necessary in preparing for the present and the future. Renewal requires that we give up what has been.

In turn, each of the gods offers another attitude. As the origin of everything that is, Brahma reminds us that all is one. In his sweet spirit of eternal youth and playful seduction, Krishna invites acceptance of joy as natural. As the goddess of troubled times, Kali makes it necessary for us to slow down enough to examine what is wrong. Demonstrating in her creative disorder how annihilation of old attitudes allows new ways, she opens us to opportunities offered by disruption.

The practical value of attending to these changing gods is implicit in the attitudes each god models. Making use of this instruction requires recognition of the nature of our changing situations and willingness to serve each god in turn.

New learning always has its dangers. Each new attitude is open to abuse. In social and political terms, at its best the loving call of Krishna's flute is exemplified in the dedicated, devotional leadership and nonviolent following of Martin Luther King, Jr. At its worst the melody is misused in the mindless devotion of blissed-out Moonies, whose entrancement ignores all else, and of the Moral Majority, whose belief in an ideal is expressed as hatred of anything different.

At her best, Kali's sword inspires militant leaders as committed and courageous as Malcolm X. Corruption of the constructive aspects of her onslaught inspires nihilistic punk rockers and terrorists so tied to destruction that they leave no room for the renewals required for allowing an improved and easier order.

In Western thought, the concept of Providence comes closest to Hindus contending constructively with Kali. Jews and Christians must also try to make sense of the pointless suffering in this world of constancy and change. They attribute to God's grand design, the unfairness of a life filled with the pain of apparently undeserved losses and disappointments. Senseless pain is justified as sensible punishment for sin, as education for the victim (or as an object lesson for others), as a test of faith, or as the stigmata of sacrificial selection for a heavenly afterlife.

The Western secular ideal of progress is like the Hindu commitment to Krishna. The former's assumptions are that humankind's lot is gradually improving toward greater happiness through the advancement of technology and the gradual improvement of human nature. Marx, Darwin, and Teilhard de Chardin all imagined cosmic change working toward the increasing perfection.

Despite the apparent contradictions evident in the adversity of centuries of poverty, plague, prejudice, and war, these Utopians insisted that every day in every way, things were getting better. If secular Nirvana was delayed by samsara, it was only because temporarily these ideals had been corrupted and misused. For a long time, my own immersion in the failed ideals of Providence and progress left me despairing and disillusioned.

I am happier having given up my fatalistically pessimistic vision in favor of accepting life subject to chance rolls of the dice. I can cope with its contradictions when I attend to the attitudinal models best suited to meeting each unexpected change. At times I still find it too difficult to let go of one god so that another may be served. Remaining helplessly stuck in the unsettling gap occurring at the time of the changing of the gods, I leave myself needlessly vulnerable.

During these transitions, I am often unprepared for making as much as I might of opportunities for happier experiences. As sweet with promise as those times may be, unless I become sufficiently conscious of Krishna, I am unable to ease into more relaxed and playful ways of enjoying time spent with the people I love most. Guarding against danger of troubled times already past makes it difficult to drop my characteristic Shiva/Kali defenses of detachment and disruption.

At those times, reorientation to yet another Eastern outlook offers the release from the sorrows of samsara that I need to immerse myself in the joys of Nirvana. At the crossroads of contradictions, stubbornly stalwart people like myself find it useful to try the left-handed path of tantra.[1] In dealing with recalcitrant attitudes, tantra teaches: When you can't give up, give in! Continue doing what you do. As time passes, the contradictions will coalesce.

Tantric practices sound simple, but they are not easy. The central theme is that *like cures like*. When we surrender to our weaknesses, stumbling blocks can be turned into stepping-stones. Poison is an antidote to poison. A thorn can be used to remove a thorn. This medieval Indian mysticism evolved as a way of instructing those who could not say "no" to temptation. Tantra taught an attitude of devotion in which saying "yes" to forbidden desires could make sinning sacred.

Tantra encouraged worshipers of Shiva when they felt stuck to indulge the very impulses they sought to overcome. Nothing was prohibited. Everything was allowed. Paradoxically, detached striving for perfection was turned toward passionate pursuit of imperfection.

Opposites united, turning Kali's destructive disruption into Krishna's seductive devotion.

In both the Hindu and Buddhist practice of Yoga, the aspirant must make certain painful sacrifices in the pursuit of spiritual liberation. Religious rules of conduct require transcending the distractions of the flesh. It is as difficult for the psychotherapy patient to give up the comforts of psychological resistances as it is for the yogi to overcome carnal temptations. Should the guru or the therapist push the disciple or the patient to get on with it, a power struggle ensues that only increases the distracting behaviors.[2]

In the practice of Yoga, tantra is a "left-handed" approach that works by transforming attachments into new ways of attaining spiritual awareness. The previously forbidden acts of eating, drinking, and sexual practices become the sacramental fare of tantric rites. The guru guides the devotee in participating in the forbidden acts. Once transformed, they are no longer acts of attachment to the flesh. Carried out in a state of controlled consciousness, they become acts of devotion in the service of spiritual illumination.

The psychotherapist can bring this same spirit of sacred carnival to meeting patient-induced impasses. The psychotherapeutic technique that parallels tantra is called paradox. Like tantra, paradox transforms antitherapeutic resistances into the very consciousness from which they previously served to distract.

The therapist uses paradox as a way of accepting and redefining the patient's avoidant behavior. The patient is instructed to continue to do what he or she is already doing. Going along with the therapist's instructions, the patient participates in the therapeutic alliance. Resisting the instructions requires giving up the countertherapeutic behavior. In either event, paradox redefines the meaning of the patient's behavior so that avoidance itself becomes a form of patient participation. Emphasis is shifted away from struggle to control the patient to the redefinition of the therapeutic relationship.

There are three basic paradoxical instructions:

1. "Continue to do exactly what you are doing."
2. "Do even more of what you are already doing."
3. "Know that the meaning of what you are doing is the exact opposite of what you believe it to be."

I used the first type of paradoxical instruction with a patient who was repeatedly distracted whenever we began to speak about his feelings about his mother. At such times, his focus of attention shifted to the sounds of birds singing outside the office window, of trash-removal trucks in the parking lot, and of the distant sirens of passing emergency vehicles.

He accepted my interpretation that this was his way of avoiding his anxiety about his relationship with his mother, but he insisted that unfortunately there was nothing he could do about it. I agreed, and suggested it was crucial that he continue to be distracted for a while.

My paradoxical instructions were: "Any time the topic of your mother comes up, you are to pay complete attention to whatever sounds you hear coming from outside the office window. Whenever this happens, you will know, 'This is the way I can avoid thinking about Mother!' "

The exaggeration demanded by the second type of paradoxical instruction is best suited to measurable avoidant behaviors such as chronic lateness. It proved useful with a man I had been seeing for several weeks; he came to every session *exactly* ten minutes late. When I pointed this out he acknowledged feeling upset about this uncontrollable behavior. He admitted that no matter what kind of appointment he had, he was always ten minutes late.

Though precise in his imprecision, this master of *un*punctuality experienced himself as helpless to do anything about his behavior. He understood that it cost him one fifth of his therapy time but took no responsibility for what he was doing. Because he considered this ten-minute tardiness to be a neurotic symptom, he was able to come late without feeling that he had chosen to do so.

I told him that if he instructed me to do so, I would arrange for him to cure himself of this symptom. He was hesitantly enthusiastic when I suggested that for our next session he should plan to come *fifteen* minutes late. He balked at the idea of wasting five minutes. I assured him that by risking these five minutes he might eventually be able to save the time usually wasted by his symptom of chronic lateness.

For the next session he arrived fifteen minutes late. He was furious about having to wait for those last five minutes. The paradoxical experience soon stopped his coming late. It also allowed him to recognize the secret hostile power that he unconsciously fantasized wielding over those who waited for him.

The third type of paradoxical instruction involves redefining the meaning of the avoidant behavior. One young woman who was very frightened by any experience of personal intimacy always followed any closeness between us by equal time for withdrawal. The first few weeks of our working together was characterized by dramatic alternations of contact and distancing.

In any given session, she might feel safe enough to be personally revealing. At those times she was able to increase her self-awareness by temporarily tolerating being vulnerable to my getting to know her. Invariably, in our next meeting she would chat about superficial matters. During those intervening sessions her inner feelings were never revealed either to me or to herself.

Despite my pointing out and interpreting her avoidant behavior, this predictable interruption of the therapeutic process continued for several weeks. We met twice a week, but it was as though she were in therapy only half the time. My more basic therapeutic interventions resulted in her being more distant. As protection against my coercive confrontations, after any contact session she was out of touch with herself even more than usual.

This defensively distancing behavior continued until I told her: "You are pulling back from me and from yourself again. At times like this it is very important that you feel free to chat about superficial things. Whenever you do, we will understand that during our previous meeting you felt so close to me and so in touch with yourself that today you need to escape. You never have to stay any closer to me than you can bear."

Later I added elaborations of the paradox by telling her, "It's very important that you be able to hide out after any session in which you have come to know more about yourself. Whenever you do this you will be telling me that you feel very close to me and that you are on the threshold of learning even more about yourself. It is so frightening for you to become more aware of what is going on that for a while the only way you will be able to show how close to me you feel will be by shifting into your chatty pose."

Her words denied what I said about her, but her smile confirmed my observations. Soon she began to acknowledge that her chatting must mean that she still felt open to what had gone on between us in the previous session. Gradually this alternation between vulnerability and self-protection narrowed into shifts of behavior within a given session. Eventually her withdrawal was restricted to a few chatty moments of assuring herself that she could draw back whenever she wished.

A recent example of a patient's attachment to an old god also occurred during a time of transition. We had met unexpectedly in the lobby of my office building just before our scheduled psychotherapy session. Committed to Krishna, she felt hurt and rejected by my restricting our exchange to a casual greeting. Once in the session, she complained that if I loved her as she loved me, I would not have treated her so impersonally when we met in the lobby.

The intensity of these feelings was expressed in a fantasy in which we were both thrown headlong into the white-water rapids of a river. She envisioned a floating log too small to support both of us. She was outraged as she thought of my pushing her off the log to save myself.

I invited her to imagine what she might do. She said that she loved me so much more than I loved her that she would never have pushed me off the log. However, neither would she have felt free enough of her emotional attachment to me to let go of the log so that I at least might have been saved. Instead, her love was expressed in a vision of both of us holding on to the log and drowning together. Caught between Krishna and Kali, she was unable to accept an attitude change needed to cope with the contradictions. The tantric solution lay in her exaggerating her Krishna-like devotion to the point of being willing to imagine sacrificing her life for mine. Only then was she able to consider taking care of herself even if it meant destruction of her devotedly dependent attachment to our relationship. Tantric exaggeration of her consciousness of Krishna allowed her access to Kali.

A tantric therapeutic tack in the opposite direction transformed attachment from Kali to Krishna. It was precipitated by the disruption of my cotherapist's temporary absence.[3] During earlier meetings the patients usually had spent a good deal of time trying to relieve their pain by jockeying for favored positions with the therapists. The first session that the cotherapist missed was more lively. Like Daddy and the children alone in the house with Mommy away on a shopping trip, we engaged in unusually raucous play. We shared a noisy closeness free of our regular constraints. One patient seemed disturbingly uneasy, uncharacteristically brittle, and irritably ready to argue with any man in the group. Laurie was a bright, articulate, sensually lovely woman in her thirties, unhappy over the failure of her marriage and chronically deprecating of her worth as a human being. She could not say just what was wrong that day, but she longed for the cotherapist's return.

Laurie hinted at some dark secret in her past. The group was sympathetic about her burden, but no one pushed her. In an earlier session she had asked for help with "stuck feelings" toward her mother. I had suggested that she write her mother a letter, a letter she need never send. Laurie had stalled, and the group had gone on to other matters.

During the second session that the cotherapist was away, Laurie told us that the prior meeting had been a panicky ordeal that plummeted her back into earlier experience of her mother's unavailability. She had finally written her letter to her mother. Laurie wanted to read it to the group and to reveal a terrible secret.

With a hollow show of strength born of bravado, she began to read. But the wailing undertone of her voice

broke through clearly. Filled with the anguished longing of a child left too early on her own, Laurie's letter
was an outcry of hurt, bewilderment, self-blame, and
resentment. Abandoned by an absent father and neglected by an indifferent mother, in Laurie's loneliness
she had grasped for an erotic attachment to her older
brother. While she was still an early adolescent, he
died, leaving Laurie to suffer alone the secret shame of
their incestuous sexual relationship. Added to resentment toward her parents, anger at this third betrayal
increased as the letter went on. But Laurie's bitterness and
vindictiveness were not strong enough to hide her underlying feelings of helplessness and guilt.

Some members of the group responded with sympathetic support of her resentment. Laurie begged them to
hold off and to hear out the full extent of her overriding
guilt about feeling sexually possessed. She read fragments from the pages of a diary of her tortured struggle
with sexuality throughout her high-school and college
years.

It told the tale of a girl/woman who "tried so hard to
be decent" but could never refuse sex to any man or boy
who seemed at all interested in spending time with her.
In all those years, she despised herself for being out of
control. Her self-hatred deserved both her father's de-
sertion and her mother's neglect.

The old pain she sobbed out was familiar phase-
appropriate adolescent romantic strife excruciatingly
exaggerated by an inflated sense of personal shame. Members of the group thanked Laurie for sharing so much of
herself, offered comfort for her sorrow, and told her
they loved her.

It was left to me to tell her how glad I was that she
had been wise enough to have sex with her brother
through all those empty early years. At first she could

not believe that she had heard me right. The group offered only appalled silence, tempered by the uncertain hope that I knew what I was doing.

I told Laurie that though her relationship with her brother was obviously a conflict-heavy source of lingering pain, it also had been a desperate reaching out for love. Her secret struggle was a kind of dark, self-affirming vitality through which the best of her had survived.

My own personal pain was evident as I told her of my early demonic struggle against despair. As a child, it had been made clear to me that I was bad. Even in the womb, I had endangered my mother and anguished my father. Once born, I was nothing but trouble. If not for me, my good parents would have been happy. In everything I said and all I did I always managed to hurt them.

Desperate to learn to be good, I watched all the other children trying to learn to do what they did. Seeing this, my parents would say, "See how hard he tries to be good, that bad boy." By the time I reached adolescence, I gave up. It seemed that the only thing I really knew how to do was to be bad. Committed to Kali, I got to be really good at being bad. I gave up passively finding myself in trouble, and actively I began to pursue the evil urge. My flowers of evil blossomed in the fertile demimonde of drug addicts, fighting gangs, prostitutes, pimps, and hustlers. I narrowly missed the abyss of heroin, prison, and death by violence.

Laurie began to see how much we were alike. I reminded her that when we first met, I was taken with her compelling seductiveness. It was her bridge to relationship. I was grateful that she had kept alive this longing for contact. Some group members spoke of how much my own demonic residuals of toughness, outrageousness, and irreverence had been their bridge to being with me.

Others joined our confessional communion. Ray told of his secret homosexual degradation. Several of us understood his stubborn seeking of humiliation as an early promise of strength not yet unstuck. The best of him was turned in on itself, vitality without an object. How fortunate that he had found his shameful anonymous assignations rather than let that spark of life go out.

Phyllis had survived her heartbreaking loneliness, first by a pietistic immersion in a fundamentalist church, then by an impulsive ill-starred marriage to a stranger, and finally by becoming the most promiscuously available belle in the stifling small southern town in which she was trapped. We all agreed that she was one of us. Only her religiosity seemed more sinful than our delinquencies.

We were all painfully human, all glad to have survived, each a bit less lonely for being with the other. We pitied those poor lost souls who had chosen to let their dark flames die rather than fan them left-handedly. Our community of sinners burned with a black fire. If we had not shed light, at least we had kept warm and survived. With tantric devotion to Kali, we lasted long enough through troubled times to enjoy some easier living later on.

In family life as well as in therapy, tantra has taught me to go against old attitudes unsuited to newly emerging situations. Doing the opposite of what seems sensible, I find that my frenetic passion for change no longer contradicts my calm commitment to keeping things constant. When my ascetic ideals of Shiva were faced with family disorder, I used to issue Kali's command: "Time's up!"

In the absence of paradoxical exaggeration, often this only served to make matters worse. What was once a despised interruption of activity becomes a delightful invitation to irreverence as my kids kid me out of my Shiva-inflated authority. The foolishness of the old wise one yields to youthful frivolity, and we all get to have more fun.

Free of imagining that I am there to solve other people's problems, more and more I participate playfully and enjoy all that goes on in the family's times of unorganized easy living. No longer the actively interceding patriarch, as the passively and playfully indulgent grandfather I need only issue Krishna's invitation, "Keep on doing whatever you're doing. Enjoy! Enjoy!"

During the seemingly disastrous bouts of hard times, often my shortsightedness resurfaces once again, obscuring awareness that even the worst of times will pass. This loss of perspective does not serve me any better when things are going badly than it does when life goes well. Like my joy, my suffering seems as though it will never end. I lose sight of the circle of time that has been momentarily broken, unable to imagine that the onslaught of my latest "tragedy" is also only temporary. Operating in the absence of the expectation that times will someday be easy once again, I add to my upset by overlooking the advantage of opportunities offered by life's disruptions.

If it isn't one thing it's another. For a while, living is easy. Then, all at once, I'm back in trouble again. After a time, it all gets easy again. Soon there'll be more trouble. Sometimes I feel that I just can't cope with the relentless rounds of contradictions. I get so spindled in the cycle of contrary circumstances that I don't know whether to laugh or cry. First laughter and tears, then tears and laughter. One minute I feel released into a

Nirvana of joy, and the next I am once again turning on samsara's wheel of sorrow. How am I to know which god to serve, and when?

Krishna's flute calls a tune of easy enjoyment. Before I know what's happening, the music is interrupted by yet another cacophony of Kali's sword rattle of harsh necessities. And then suddenly Krishna's melody can be heard once more.

Back and forth, back and forth, situations shift as life's loom shuttles me between the warp and the woof of constancy and change. My sanity hangs by a thread, but all the while, the broken wheel of time just goes on spinning as if my personal happiness were of no particular importance.

Whenever I feel caught between Krishna and Kali, it is time to turn back to Brahma, whose game of hide-and-seek with himself creates this illusion of opposites. The grandfather has only been playing at seducing and abandoning me. Whenever I am aware of this, I no longer need to worry whether the game was won or lost.

With the passion of a gambler endlessly indulging in the crap-shoot that is my life, I will not resist risking loss of control to each unexpected change of circumstance. Sometimes I win. Sometimes I lose. Here I am, wasn't I! No Nirvana without samsara. The odds favor the house of the gods. Even so, rather than simply sit it out, I'm ready to risk another roll. For me, this ever-changing life of mine is the only game in town.

NOTES

1. Tantric Yoga is far more complex than the paradoxical aspect I have singled out for exploration in this chapter. Compare Mircea Eliade, *Yoga: Immortality and Freedom*, trans. from the French by Willard R. Trask, Bollingen Series LVI (Princeton, N.J.: Princeton University Press, 1969), pp. 200–73.

2. Sheldon Kopp, *Back to One: A Practical Guide for Psychotherapists* (Palo Alto, Calif.: Science and Behavior Books, 1977), pp. 104–7.

3. Sheldon Kopp, *The Hanged Man: Psychotherapy and the Forces of Darkness*, (Palo Alto, Calif.: Science and Behavior Books, 1975), pp. 82–88.

ABOUT THE AUTHOR

SHELDON KOPP is a psychotherapist and teacher of psychotherapy in Washington, D.C. He is the author of AN END TO INNOCENCE; IF YOU MEET THE BUDDHA ON THE ROAD, KILL HIM!; THIS SIDE OF TRAGEDY; THE NAKED THERAPIST; NO HIDDEN MEANINGS; BACK TO ONE; HANGED MAN; and EVEN A STONE CAN BE A TEACHER.

BANTAM NEW AGE BOOKS

Bantam New Age Books are for all those interested in reflecting on life today and life as it may be in the future. This important new imprint features stimulating works in fields from biology and psychology to philosophy and the new physics.

☐	25388	**DON'T SHOOT THE DOG** Karen Pryor	$3.95
☐	25344	**SUPERMIND: THE ULTIMATE ENERGY** Barbara B. Brown	$4.95
☐	24147	**CREATIVE VISUALIZATION** Shakti Gawain	$3.95
☐	24903	**NEW RULES: SEARCHING FOR SELF-FULFILLMENT IN A WORLD TURNED UPSIDE DOWN** Daniel Yankelovich	$4.50
☐	25223	**STRESS AND THE ART OF BIOFEEDBACK** Barbara Brown	$4.95
☐	24682	**THE FIRST THREE MINUTES** Steven Weinberg	$3.95
☐	20005	**MAGICAL CHILD** Joseph Chilton Pearce	$3.95
☐	25748	**ZEN/MOTORCYCLE MAINTENANCE** Robert Pirsig	$4.95
☐	20693	**THE WAY OF THE SHAMAN** Michael Harner	$3.95
☐	25437	**TO HAVE OR TO BE** Fromm	$4.50
☐	24562	**LIVES OF A CELL** Lewis Thomas	$3.95
☐	14912	**KISS SLEEPING BEAUTY GOODBYE** K. Kolbenschlag	$3.95

Prices and availability subject to change without notice.

Buy them at your local bookstore or use this handy coupon: